Keyboard shortcuts

QWERTY

Windows 10

macOS

2021

Printed on demand by Amazon

By Lucas Bozon

For this first book, I wanted to list **the best keyboard shortcuts** with a **few tips** on how to use them on the most widespread and accessible software.

Some shortcuts and tips can be found on operating systems (Windows 10 (and compatible with earlier versions: Windows 7 and 8.1 in particular) and macOS (for the most recent versions)), on software that are either paid (**Microsoft Office: Word, Excel and PowerPoint**) or free (**Web browsers, Adobe Acrobat Reader DC, YouTube, Google Drive, Docs, Sheets, Slide and Gmail**). These software or applications allow you to do word processing, calculations, professional-looking presentations and relevant research.

For each software or application, I give you the keyboard shortcut for Windows 10 on the **1st line** and for macOS on the **2nd line**. To perform a keyboard shortcut you just have to click on the keys in the **given order** with a rather short time, some keyboard shortcuts require you to lift your finger at each key (depending on the version, this is rare, I inform you about this option if one of them in this book doesn't work).

They are **essential** for **individuals** (teenagers, students, pupils, students and adults) and for **professionals** (freelancers, teachers, accountants, computer scientists, developers, policemen, military, technicians, engineers, doctors, nurses, psychologists, waiters, secretaries, lawyers...).

I'm going to make you **love** the keys that are mostly unknown and that hide in them interesting powers associated with other keys.

For several years I wondered about the usefulness of certain buttons on keyboards, I learned from time to time that changed my life, that's why I compiled all the shortcuts that I assimilated over time and that I apply daily. I offer you my feedback on the keyboard shortcuts of **basic** software and applications. The majority of people using a computer have a word processor based usage. These keyboard shortcuts will allow you to optimize your **most recurrent** movements (writing, copying data/text, deleting, modifying, moving, navigating ...), that is to say ≈**80%** of the basic movements!

Become an expert of the QWERTY keyboard. Save time in writing e-mails, documents, reports... It is always important to have the right spelling and a nice presentation. Be more efficient in the management of computer processing.

Make nice layouts, nice reports, nice contracts, nice lines of code, nice CVs, nice tables, nice presentations...

This book will allow you to **use the mouse less** while being faster and protecting your wrist. It prevents you from touching the mouse all the time. Some mouse has extra buttons that allow them to have extra functionality directly and can be set to have the same functions as a keyboard shortcut.

The keyboard shortcuts in this book are for **all levels**: especially for beginners and intermediates. The list is far from being exhaustive.

As a bonus, I give you some tips that can be used on a laptop on the **Touchpad/Pad/Trackpad** and the differences between the **image formats** we encounter daily.

I leave you pages of notes to possibly mark other keyboard shortcuts that you will discover later and that are not included in this book.

I tried to make the book **clean** and **clear** to make it as easy to remember as possible. The book is black and white inside with special paper for ecological reasons.

I would like to point out that the keyboard shortcuts in this book are normally **compatible** with many computers nowadays, with **basic settings**. Unfortunately, they may vary according to specific versions and settings. I apologize in advance if I have omitted to correct any errors in the tips I have provided in this book. To help me, but especially to help other readers, please send me a mail to my **email address** given below. I'm currently a French student, I'm sorry for any spelling mistakes I may have made, I did my best not to. Please help me to improve this book by contacting me.

If you have any **suggestions** or **recommendations** for improvement, changes to the book and additional tips to share with other readers, please let me know:

bestof.keyboard.shortcuts@gmail.com

Thank you for your **support** and **understanding**!

This book is mainly based on my **personal experience**. I have checked and completed it with "safer" sources (official sites) as they have been checked and tested many times.

Perhaps some keyboard shortcuts may come from unofficial sources but I share them with you here anyway (on macOS, the official source remains less accurate on some keyboard shortcuts and varies a lot depending on the macOS version. For Windows 10, keyboard shortcuts rarely vary and I'm more confident about their accuracy).

This book is intended to help you with keyboard shortcuts, in particular to use the mouse less. You will become so fast that the graphics card will have trouble following! I have tried to list as many tips as possible that I have been able to find and experiment with over the last few years in school and at work. I have seen among other things the lack of knowledge of some of my friends, relatives and professionals with whom I have had the chance to collaborate. They were missing out on tools that are accessible to everyone in order to be more efficient and precise in their work.

I thank you for the purchase of this book, which I hope will help you and make your life easier. It only remains for me to wish you a **good reading**!

And good test!

Summary

Classic & general shortcuts

They apply to all of the following software (in the main)
To start with the base | Windows then macOS |:

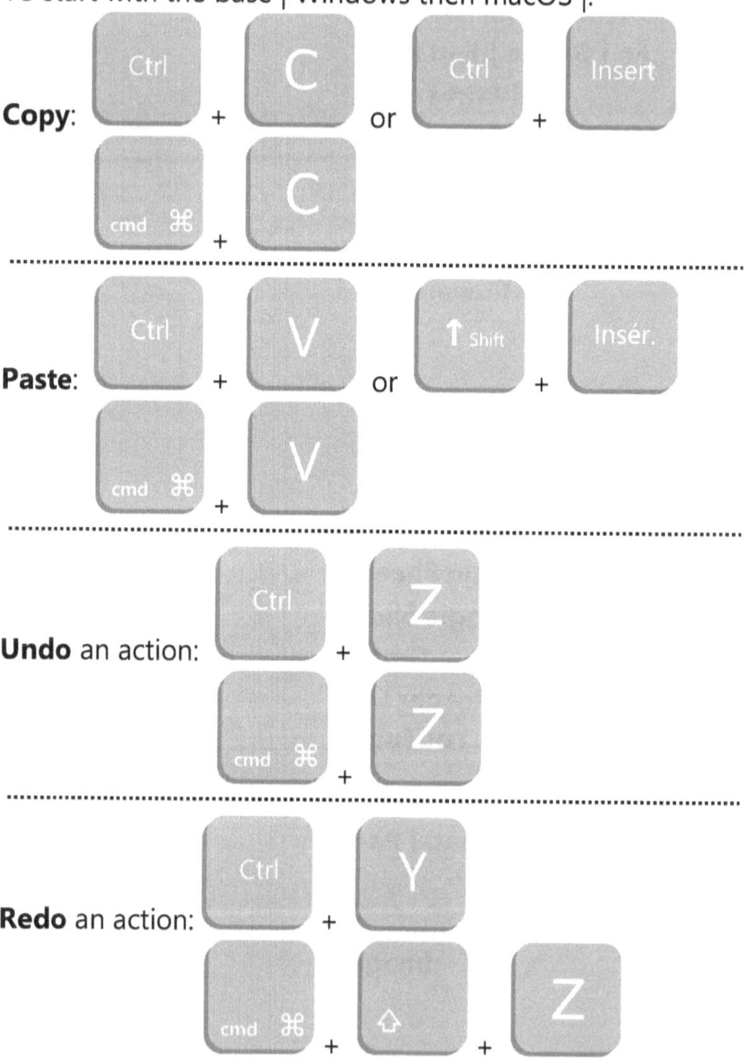

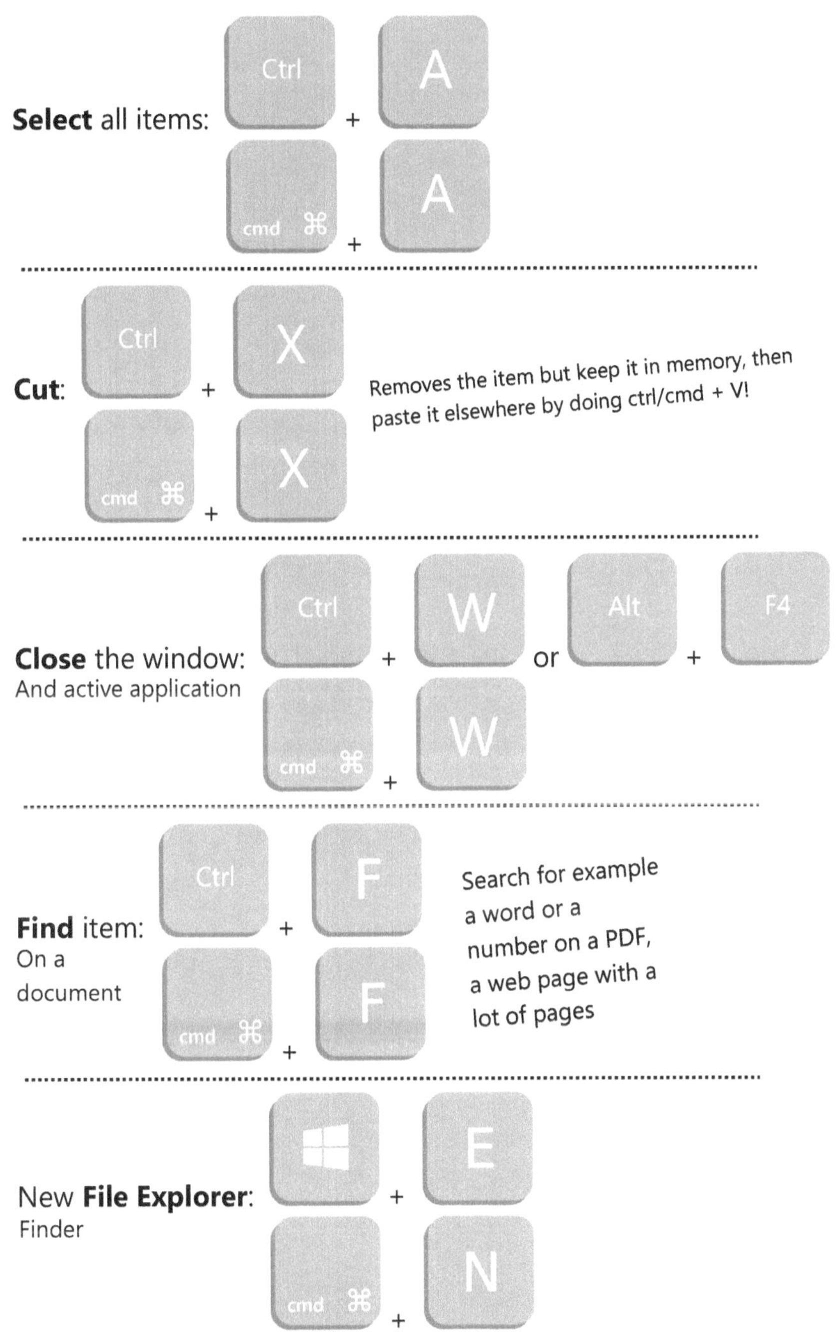

Select all items:
Ctrl + A
cmd ⌘ + A

Cut:
Ctrl + X
cmd ⌘ + X
Removes the item but keep it in memory, then paste it elsewhere by doing ctrl/cmd + V!

Close the window:
And active application
Ctrl + W or Alt + F4
cmd ⌘ + W

Find item:
On a document
Ctrl + F
cmd ⌘ + F
Search for example a word or a number on a PDF, a web page with a lot of pages

New File Explorer:
Finder
⊞ + E
cmd ⌘ + N

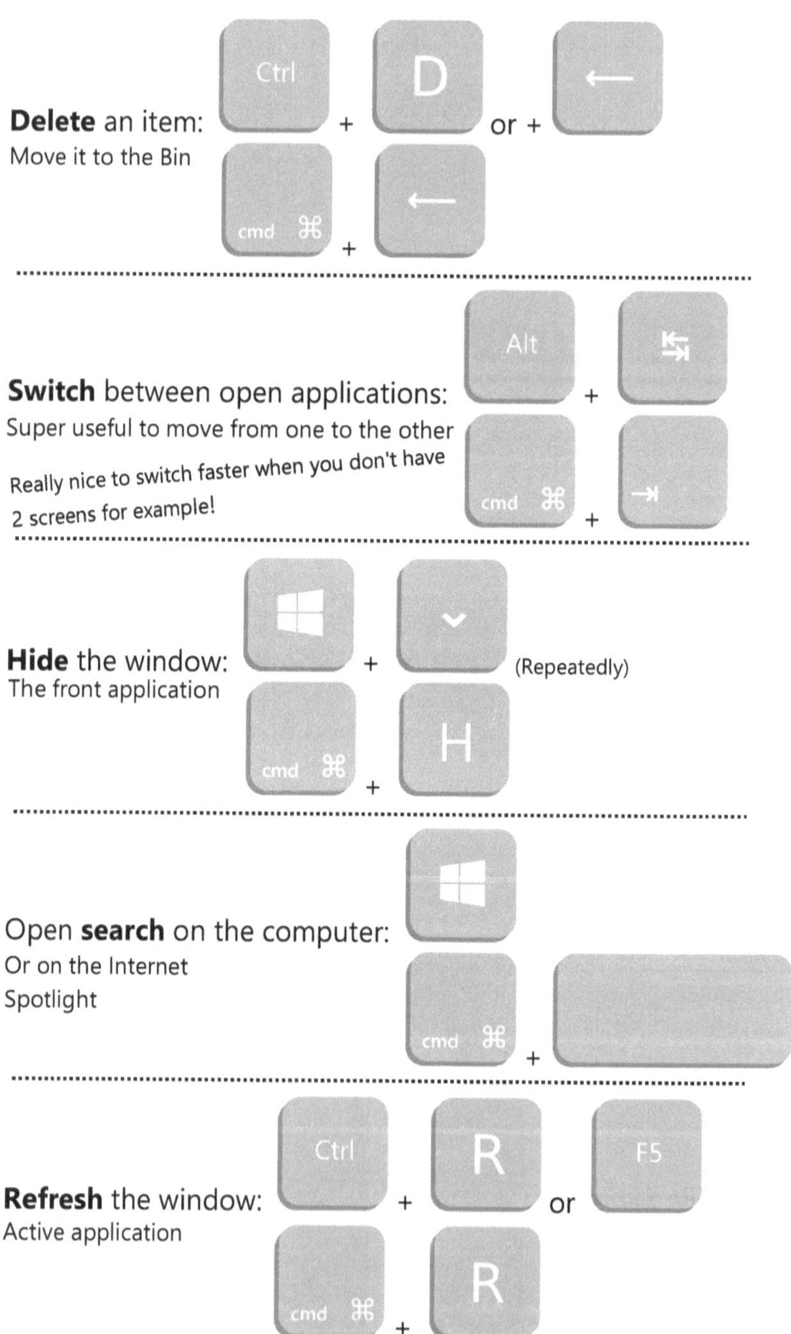
Delete an item:
Move it to the Bin
Ctrl + D or + ←
cmd ⌘ + ←

Switch between open applications:
Super useful to move from one to the other
Really nice to switch faster when you don't have
2 screens for example!
Alt +
cmd ⌘ +

Hide the window:
The front application
+ (Repeatedly)
cmd ⌘ + H

Open search on the computer:
Or on the Internet
Spotlight
cmd ⌘ +

Refresh the window:
Active application
Ctrl + R or F5
cmd ⌘ + R

Take a **screenshot**:
Whole screen

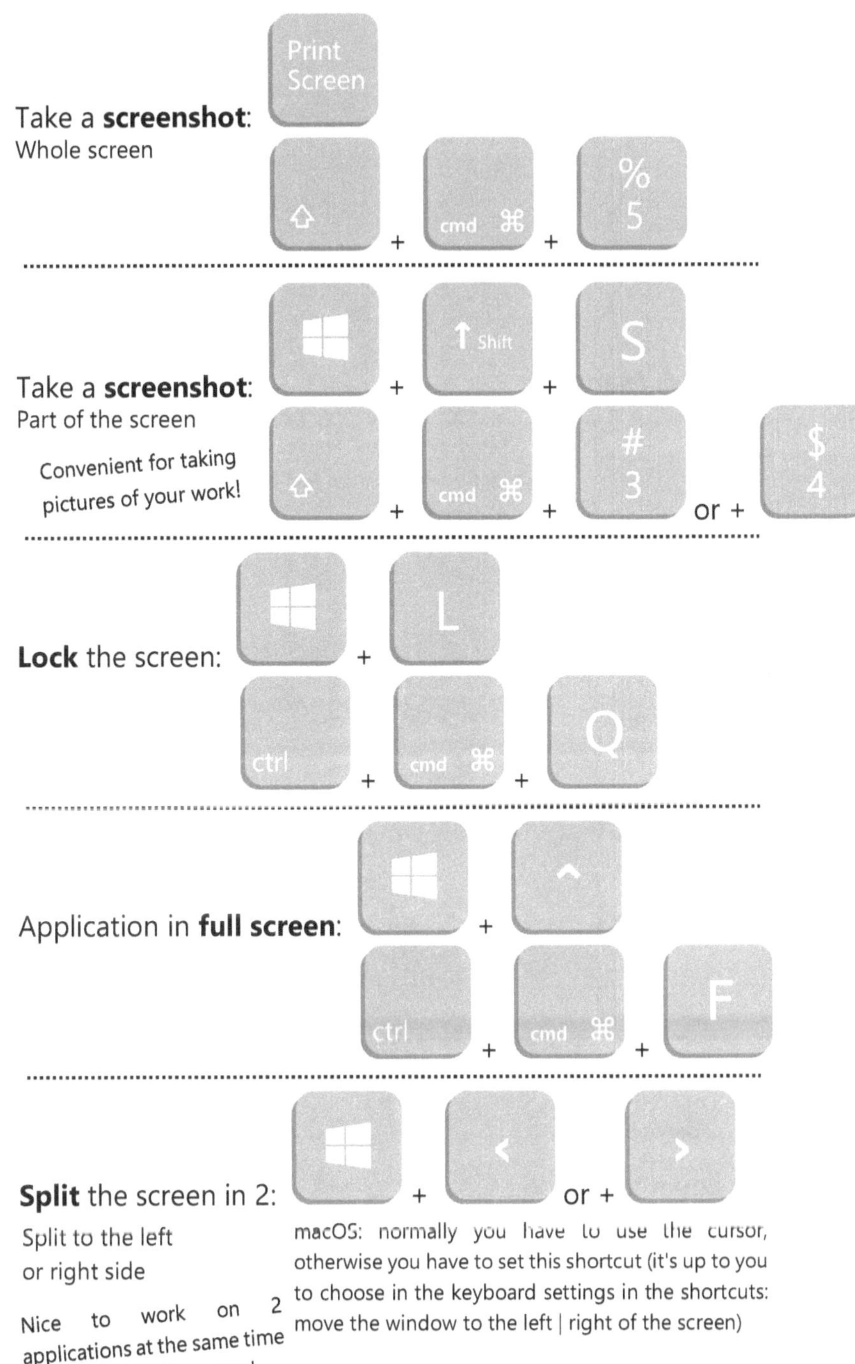

Take a **screenshot**:
Part of the screen

Convenient for taking
pictures of your work!

Lock the screen:

Application in **full screen**:

Split the screen in 2:

Split to the left
or right side

Nice to work on 2
applications at the same time
without having 2 screens!

macOS: normally you have to use the cursor,
otherwise you have to set this shortcut (it's up to you
to choose in the keyboard settings in the shortcuts:
move the window to the left | right of the screen)

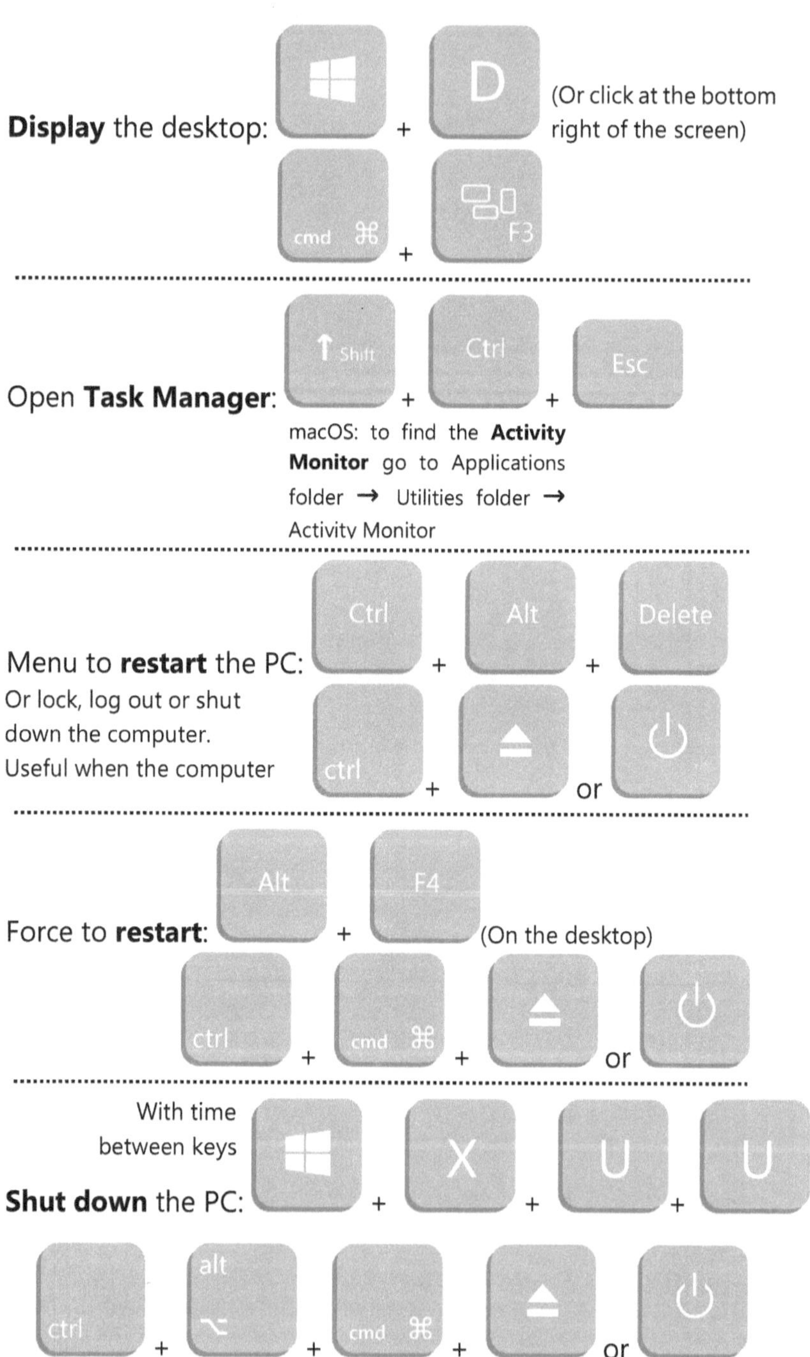

Display the desktop:
+
(Or click at the bottom right of the screen)
cmd ⌘
+
F3

Open Task Manager:
↑ Shift
+
Ctrl
+
Esc
macOS: to find the Activity Monitor go to Applications folder → Utilities folder → Activity Monitor

Menu to restart the PC:
Ctrl
+
Alt
+
Delete
Or lock, log out or shut down the computer.
Useful when the computer
ctrl
+
or

Force to restart:
Alt
+
F4
(On the desktop)
ctrl
+
cmd ⌘
+
or

With time between keys
Shut down the PC:
+
X
+
U
+
U
ctrl
+
alt
+
cmd ⌘
+
or

Open **Task view**:
On all desktops
Mission control

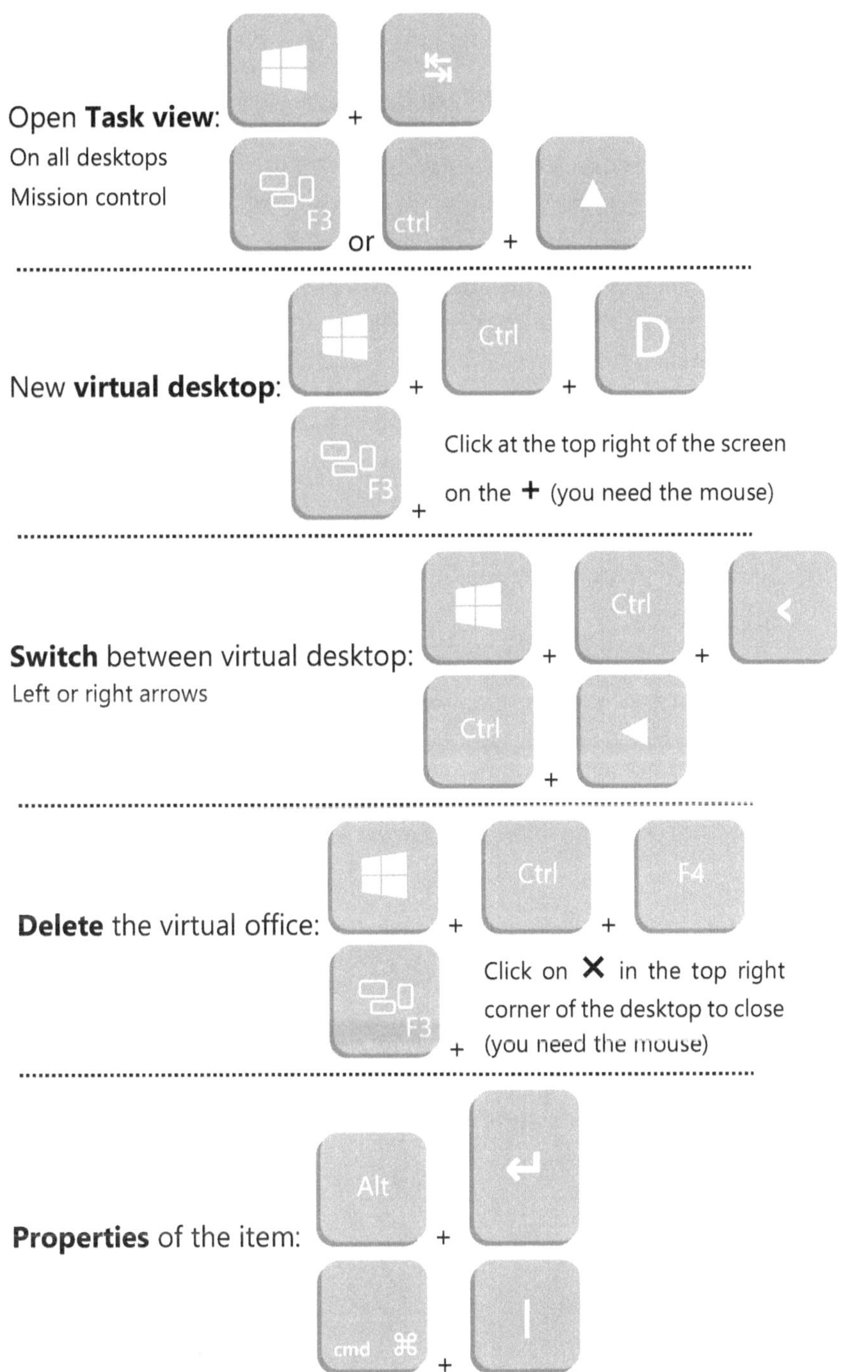

New **virtual desktop**:

Switch between virtual desktop:
Left or right arrows

Delete the virtual office:

Properties of the item:

Shortcuts on all software

Emoji | Special characters

To make **special characters** on Windows 10 and MacOS, there are some shortcuts to know to make beautiful documents and not make mistakes. They are unfortunately **not directly accessible** due to lack of space. These shortcuts are really useful to make for example a nice professional letter, a nice presentation, clean and well finished paragraphs and text zones. There are **several ways** to make these characters, I give you several of them.

Windows 10:

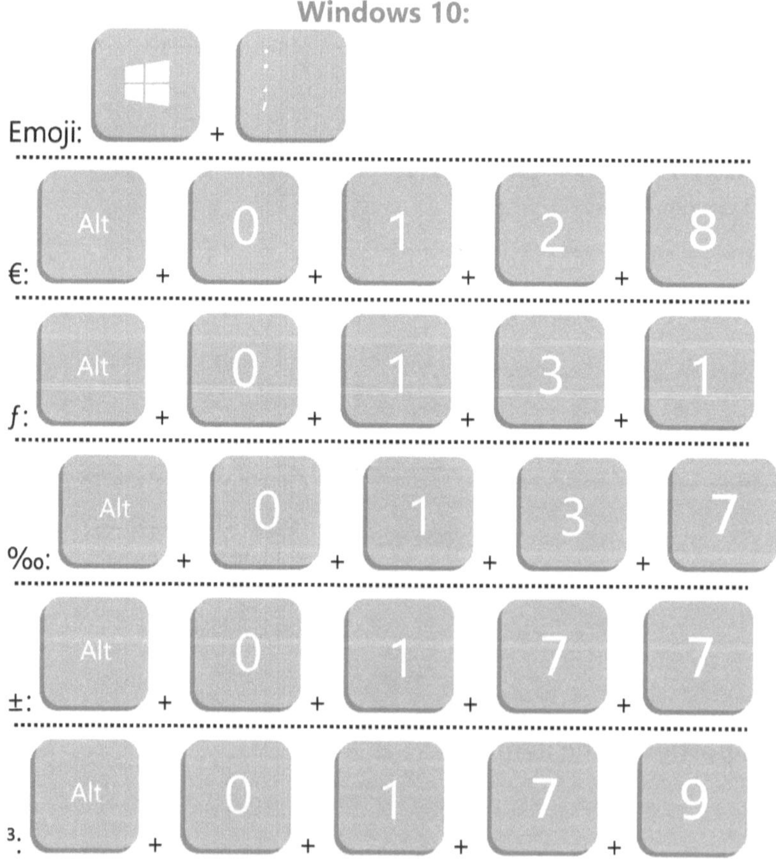

Emoji: [⊞] + [;]

€: [Alt] + [0] + [1] + [2] + [8]

ƒ: [Alt] + [0] + [1] + [3] + [1]

‰: [Alt] + [0] + [1] + [3] + [7]

±: [Alt] + [0] + [1] + [7] + [7]

³: [Alt] + [0] + [1] + [7] + [9]

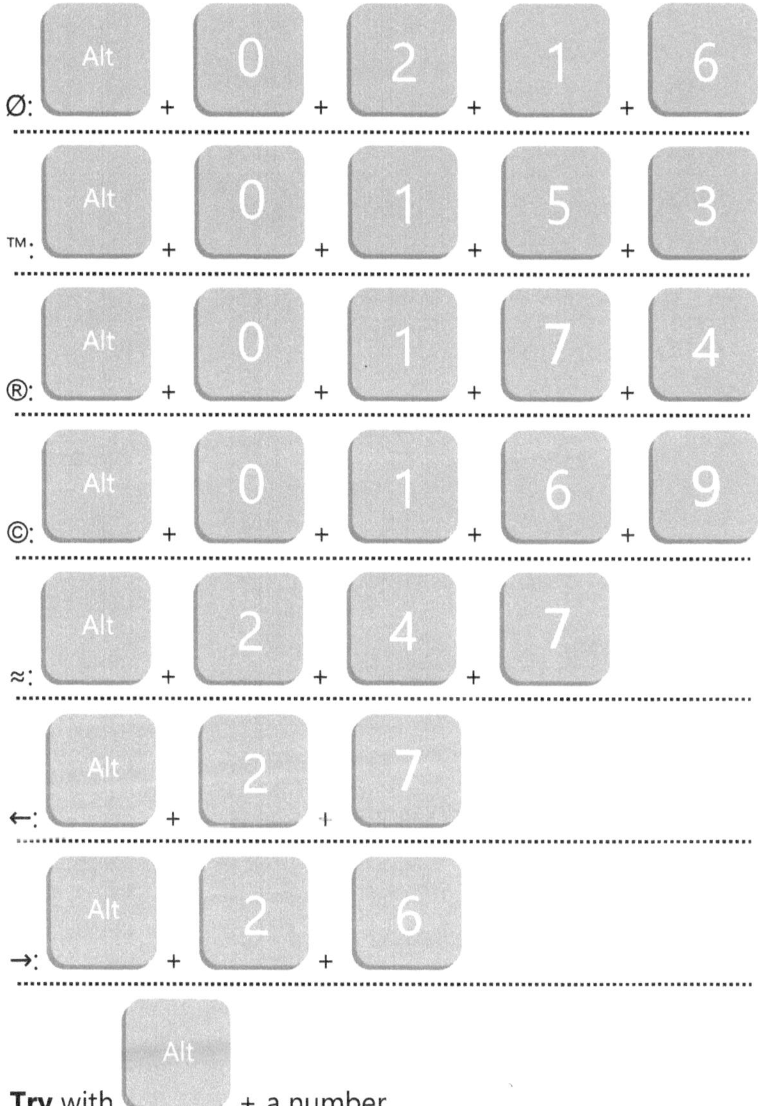

Try with Alt + a number

macOS:

Emoji: 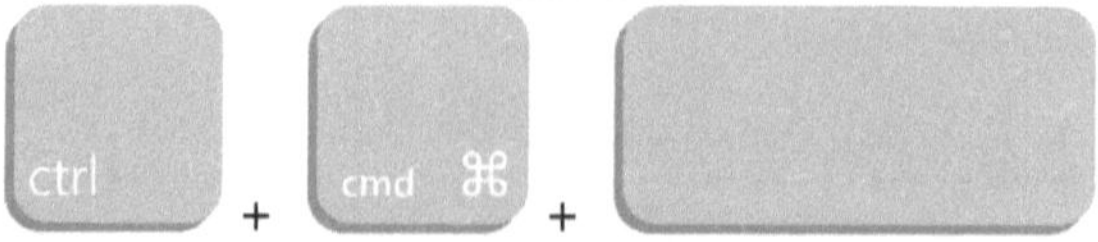 ctrl + cmd ⌘ +

€: alt + ⇧ + @ 2

ƒ: alt + F

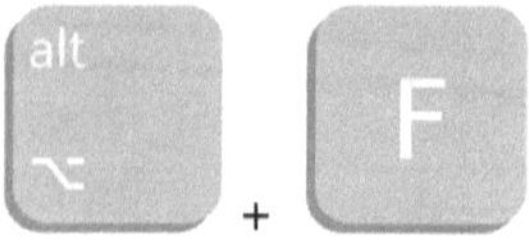

‰: alt + ⇧ + R

±: alt + ⇧ + + =

Ø: alt + ⇧ + O

To have accent on a letter **press** and **hold** the letter you want and a **pop-up** will appear and you will choose the accent you want.

ƒ: alt + F

™: alt + @ 2

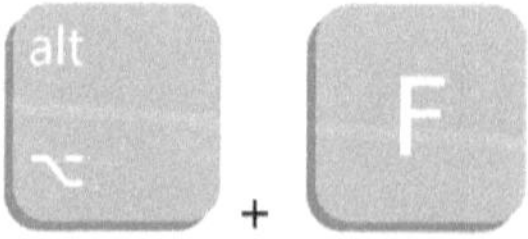

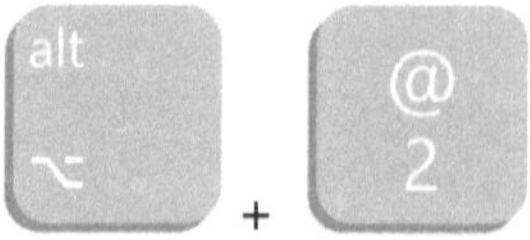

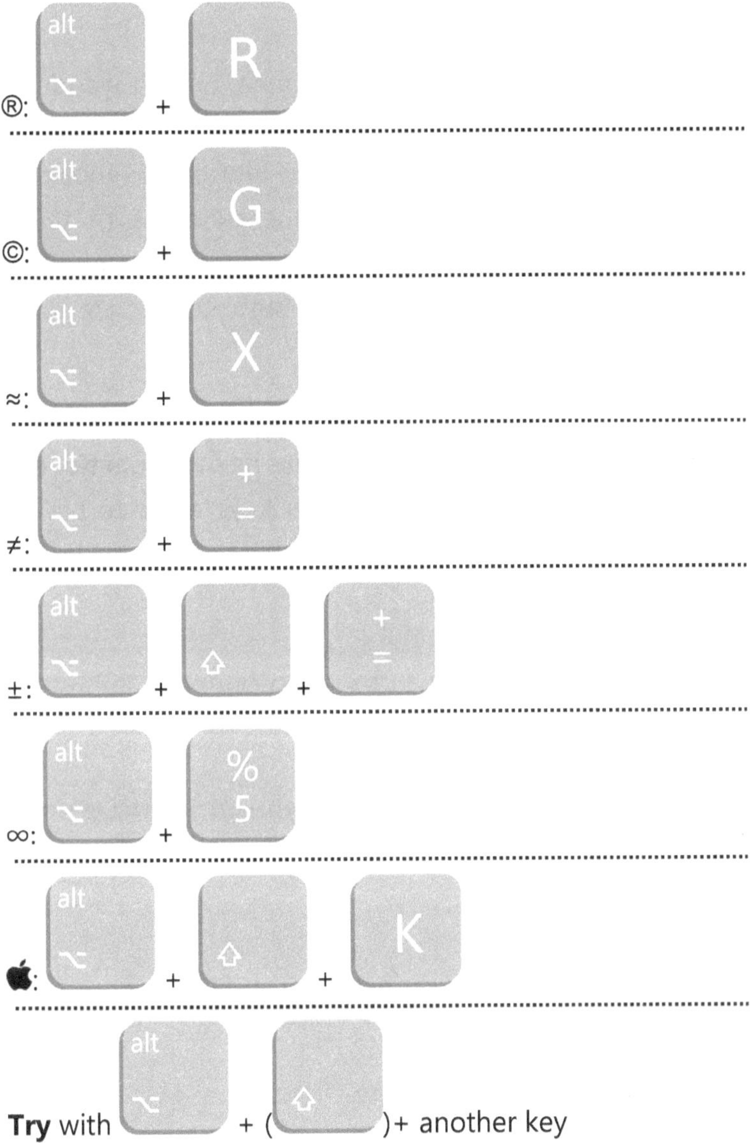

alt
R
®: +
alt
G
©: +
alt
X
≈: +
alt
+ =
≠: +
alt
+ =
±: + ⇧ +
alt
% 5
∞: +
alt
K
: + ⇧ +
alt
⇧
Try with + ( )+ another key

Function | Fn

I ignored this function key for a long time, I didn't wonder about the usefulness of some keys like this one. So, either you are attached to the people who live in this ignorance or you live while being conscious of the existence of this mysterious key. It is not present on all keyboards, only on keyboards that don't have **2 rows of keys** to separate the functions.

Quite simply, it allows **access to the functions** present next to the F1 to F12 keys. Each keyboard has its **own functions**. Each F1, F2...F12 key, along with other keys, allow to have keyboard shortcuts, but the functionalities on these keys (often in the same color **Fn** (**Windows 10**) and **fn** (**macOS**)) allow to have keyboard shortcuts for **sound, brightness, sleep and other very practical** features especially on laptops.

Delete

To delete "normally", i.e. to the left of the cursor, the basic key is available on the keyboard. But to **delete to the right of the cursor**, there is a solution that is not known to

everyone on **Windows 10** with the key 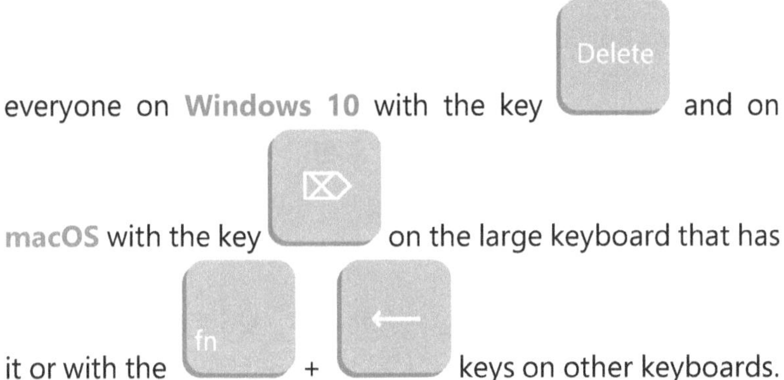 and on macOS with the key on the large keyboard that has it or with the fn + keys on other keyboards.

The purpose of this book is to familiarize you with your keyboard and mouse. This part is more of a trick than a keyboard shortcut, but it is interesting on spreadsheets or text boxes. The key or allows you to go to **the end of the line, the text zone and the page** for example. As for the key or , it allows you to go to **the beginning of the line, the text zone and the page** in the opposite way to the previous key. These keys **avoid having to click several times** on the small arrows on the left or right, but also the top and bottom arrows. They also **replace the mouse** and the back and forth movement of the wrist.

Tabulation | Tab

This key is used to perform **various actions**. To begin with, it allows you to make **an indent** at the beginning of paragraphs.  (Windows 10) (macOS)

On forms, text fields/multiple boxes during a registration for example, this key allows you to **move from one box to the next**, thus avoid having to use the mouse over and over again. To return to the previous box:

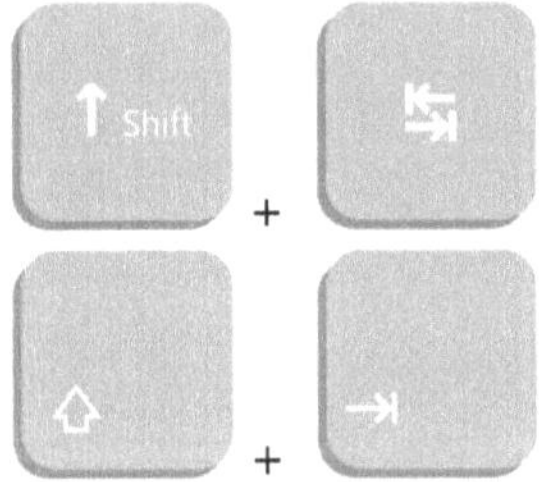

On the different applications and most of software that propose word **suggestions**, **automatic login** or **password**; when you simply mark a few letters or numbers, the Tab key allows you to **complete** and **write** the suggestion **instantly**. On the pages of web browsers, it allows you to move from one **hyperlink** to another.

I've already mentioned this keyboard shortcut, but it **changes my life** so much, it's very appreciated by **gamers**, it allows you to **switch** from one window to the other:

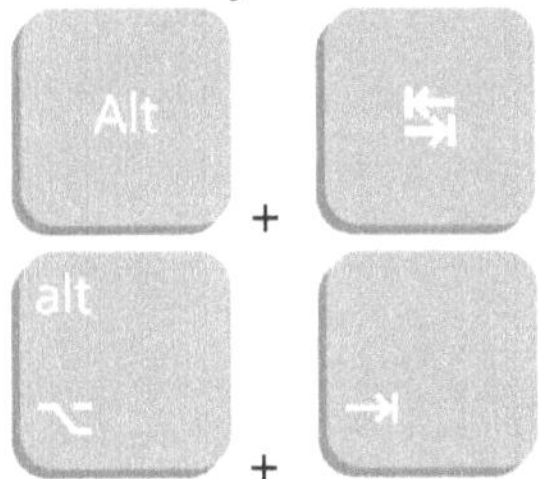

Click on the mouse wheel

This is another trick to **navigate/swipe** smoothly on all applications, open a **new page** from a link (hyperlink, a site ...). You simply have to click on the mouse wheel (if it has one): (on some laptops a small button replaces this wheel).

On all the applications, click on the wheel and **drag it up or down**, you can go up and down at **your own pace**. This way you can scroll **precisely**.

On **hyperlinks** (these links allow you to send you to another document, in fact, it links to another document and by clicking on it opens the other document automatically), links from sites on web browsers, clicking on the mouse wheel **avoids a set of keys** (ctrl + right click or right click + tab: open the page in a new tab). Thus, this click allows to open a **new tab** without leaving the active page, or to **close a tab** without clicking on the red cross.

With practice, this trick is really **practical** and **simplifies** your life!

Here are the keyboard shortcuts to use on the **3 following Microsoft Office software**, with the **generals** seen at the beginning of the book:

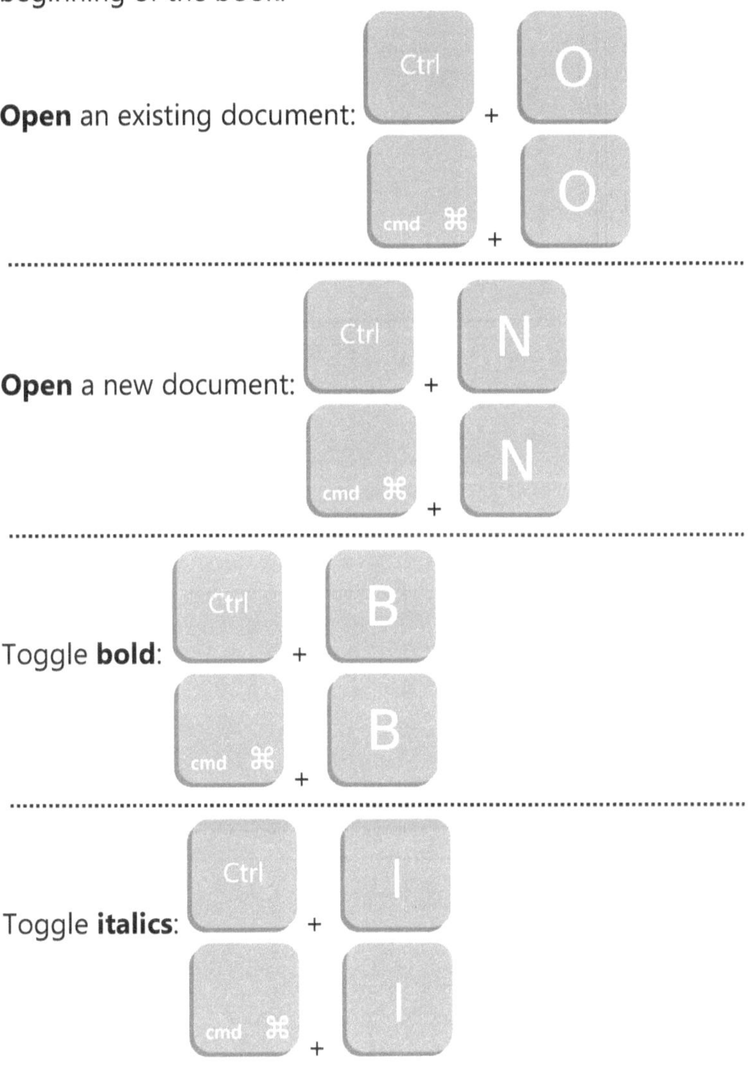

Open an existing document:

Open a new document:

Toggle **bold**:

Toggle **italics**:

Toggle **underscore**:

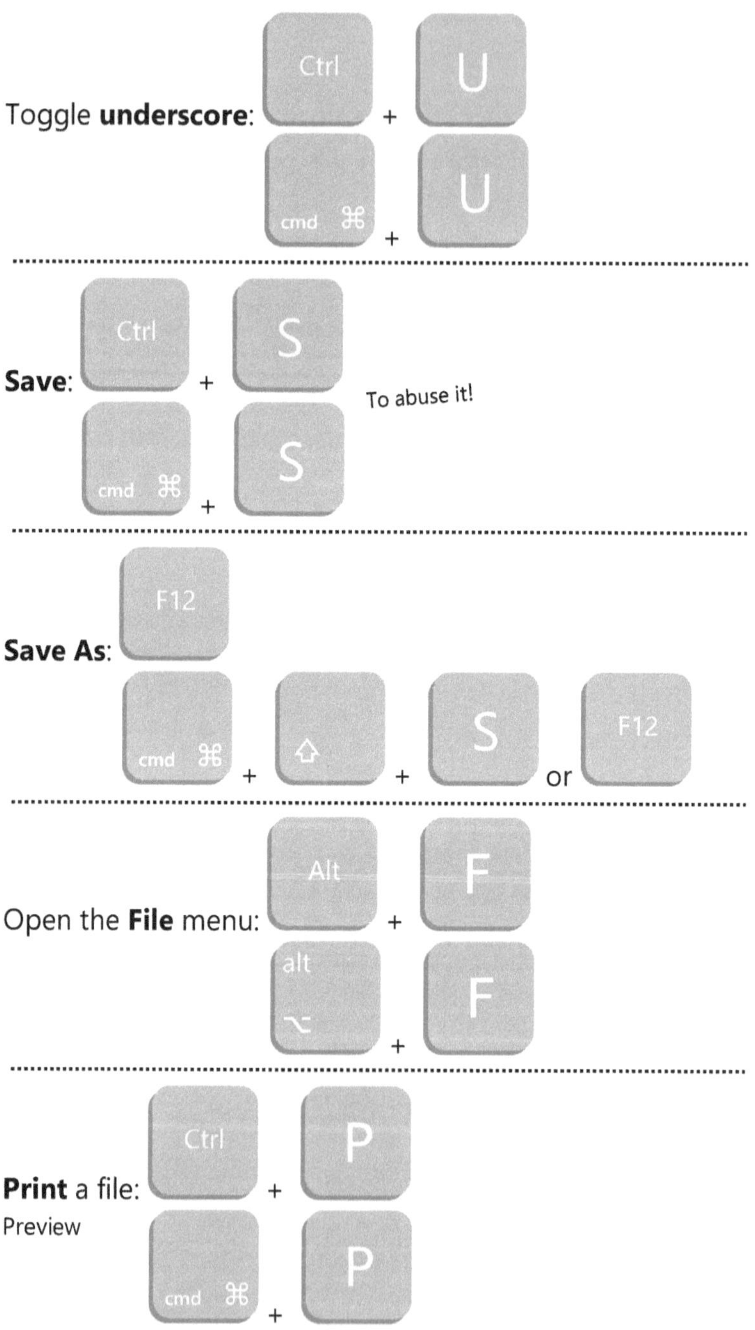

Save:

Save As:

Open the **File** menu:

Print a file:

Preview

Word | .docx

The following keyboard shortcuts will be, for the most part, similar to those for **Libre Office Writer**. They are the **reference word processing** software. To better know and master them, I propose some vital keyboard shortcuts.

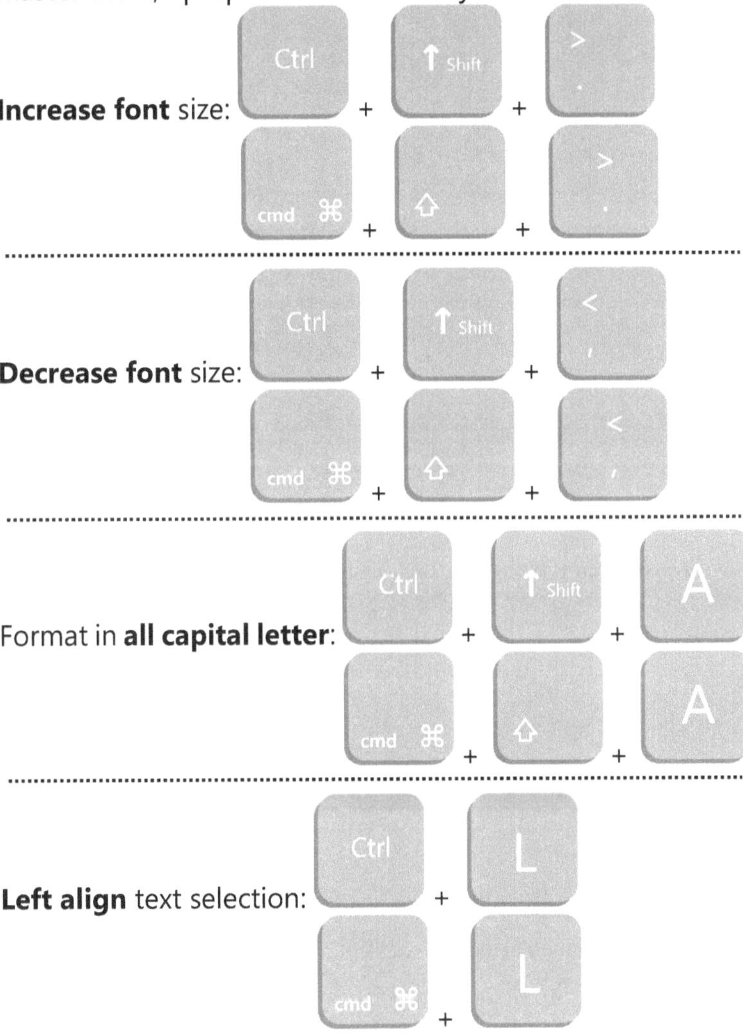

Increase font size:

Decrease font size:

Format in **all capital letter**:

Left align text selection:

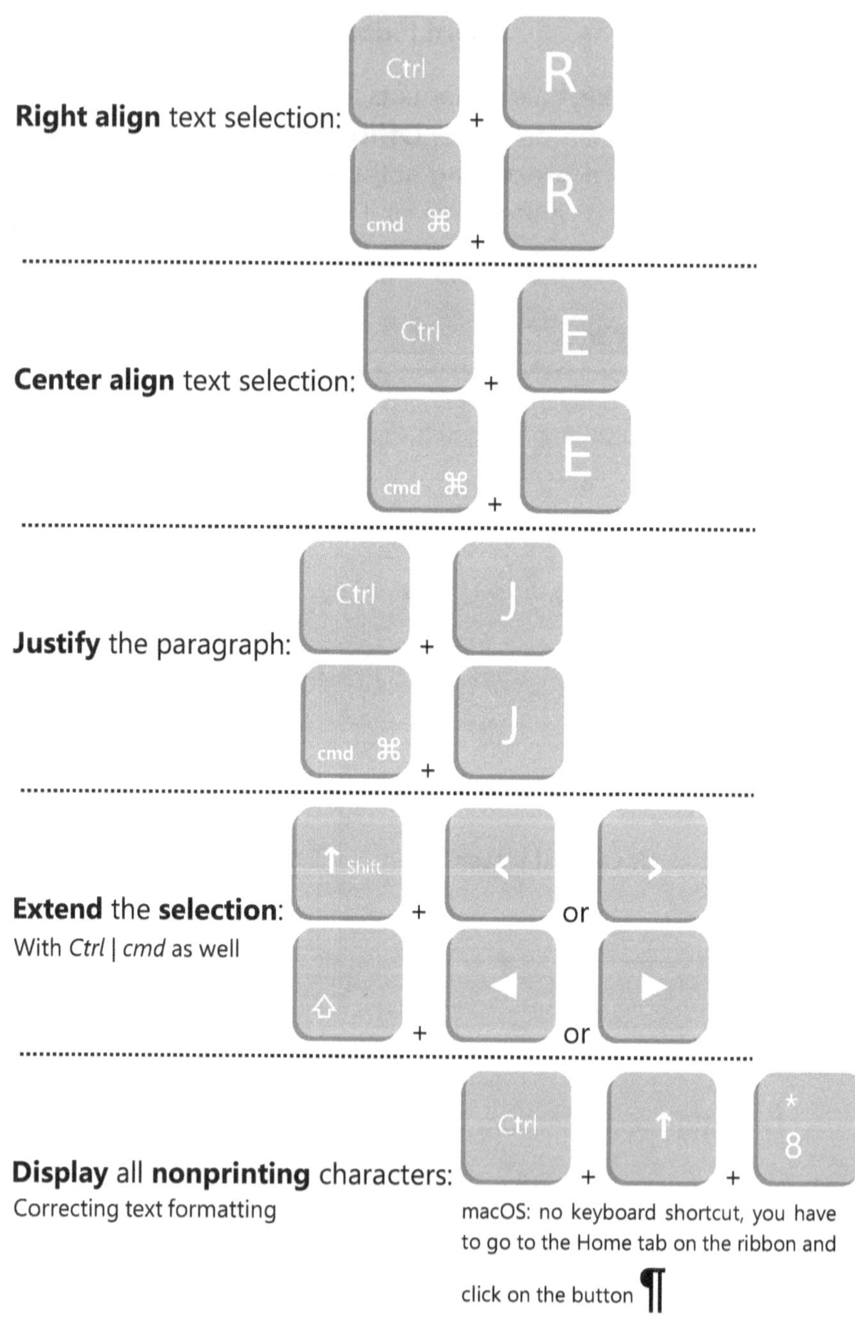

Right align text selection:

Center align text selection:

Justify the paragraph:

Extend the **selection**:
With *Ctrl | cmd* as well

Display all **nonprinting** characters:
Correcting text formatting

macOS: no keyboard shortcut, you have to go to the Home tab on the ribbon and click on the button ¶

Insert a page **break**: 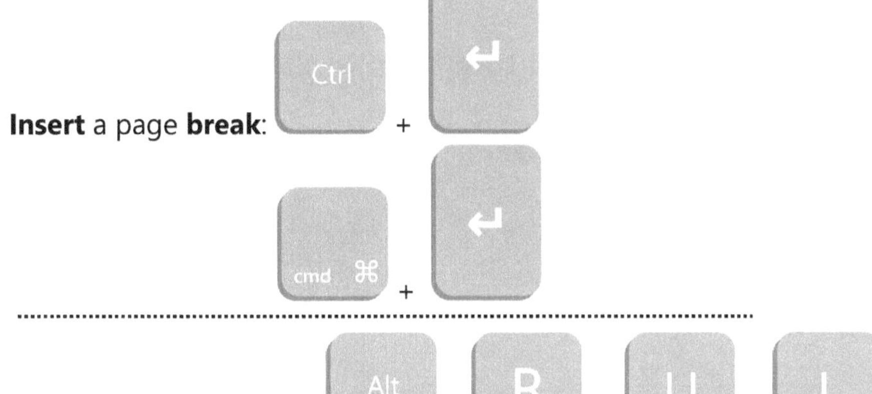 Ctrl + ↵

cmd ⌘ + ↵

Set **Proofing Language**: Alt + R + U + L

For automatic correction

macOS: no keyboard shortcut, you have to go to the Review tab on the ribbon, click on the Language button and choose in the drop-down menu Set Proofing Language...

<h1 style="text-align:center">Excel | .xlsx</h1>

Libre Office Calc will have, on the whole, the same keyboard shortcuts as those that follow. This 2 **very complete** software are **calculation tools** at the **heart of various activities**, the use varies enormously according to your **profile**. That's why I've grouped together the main keyboard shortcuts to master **mathematics** in particular. Namely that Excel is full of keyboard shortcuts!

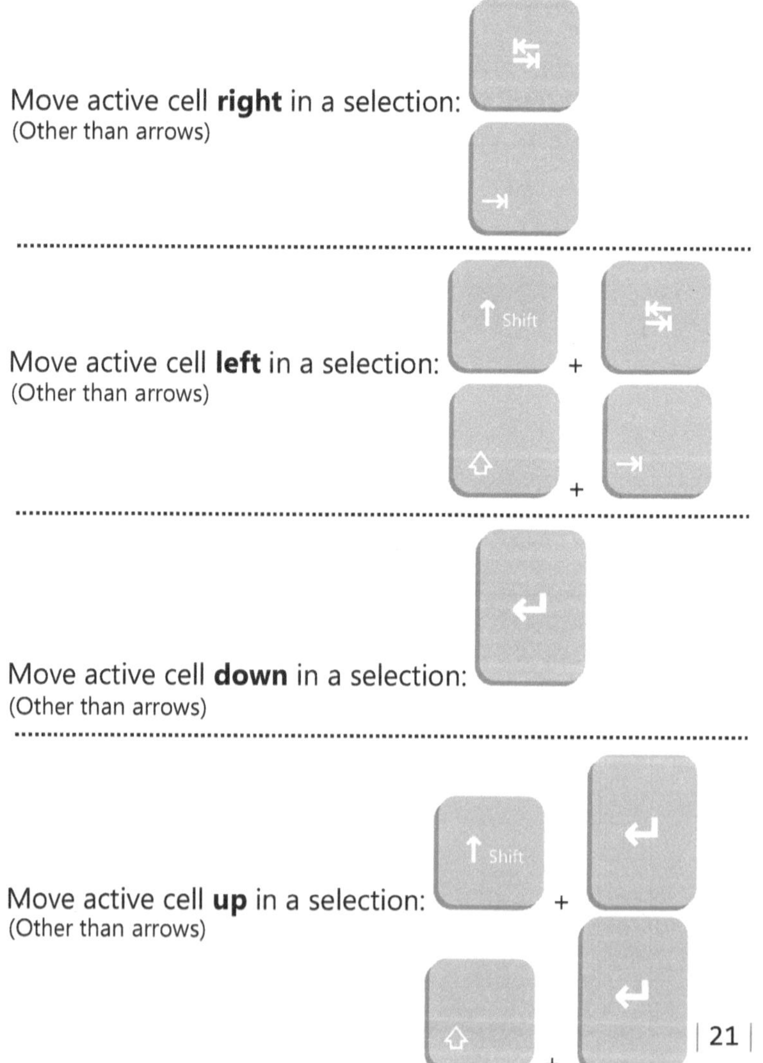

Move active cell **right** in a selection:
(Other than arrows)

Move active cell **left** in a selection:
(Other than arrows)

Move active cell **down** in a selection:
(Other than arrows)

Move active cell **up** in a selection:
(Other than arrows)

Little trick to adjust the **column** or the **line** to the text: double click on the line separating 2 columns or 2 lines when this **arrow** is displayed:

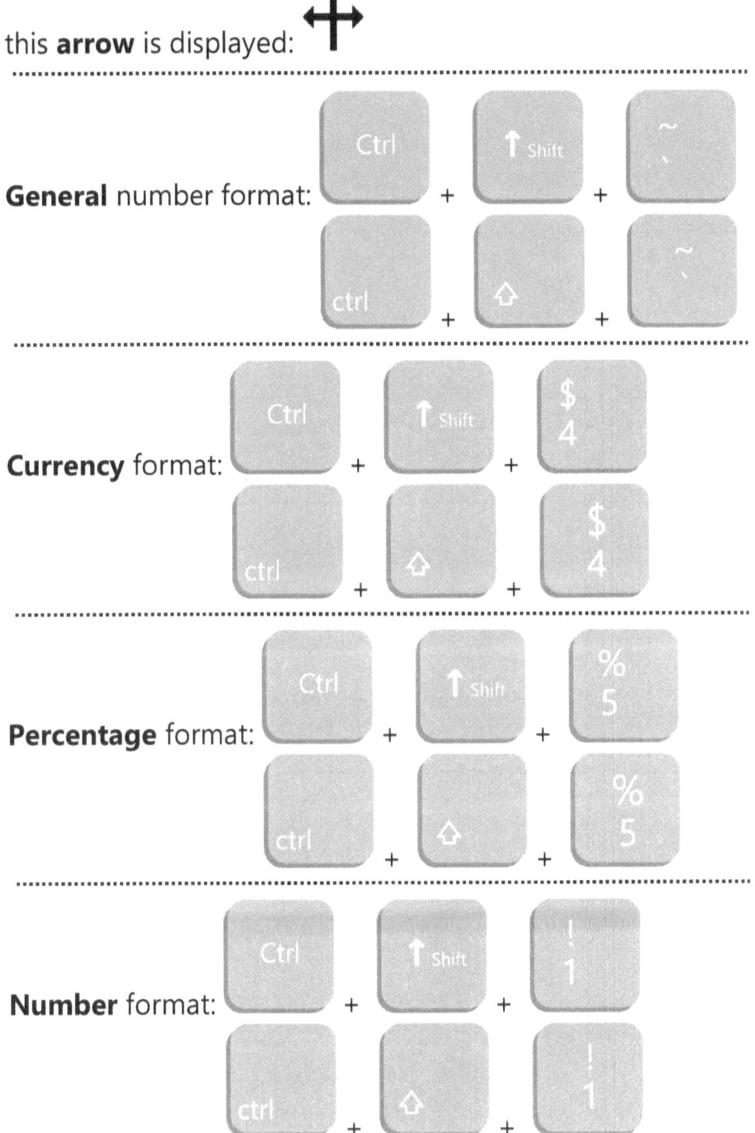

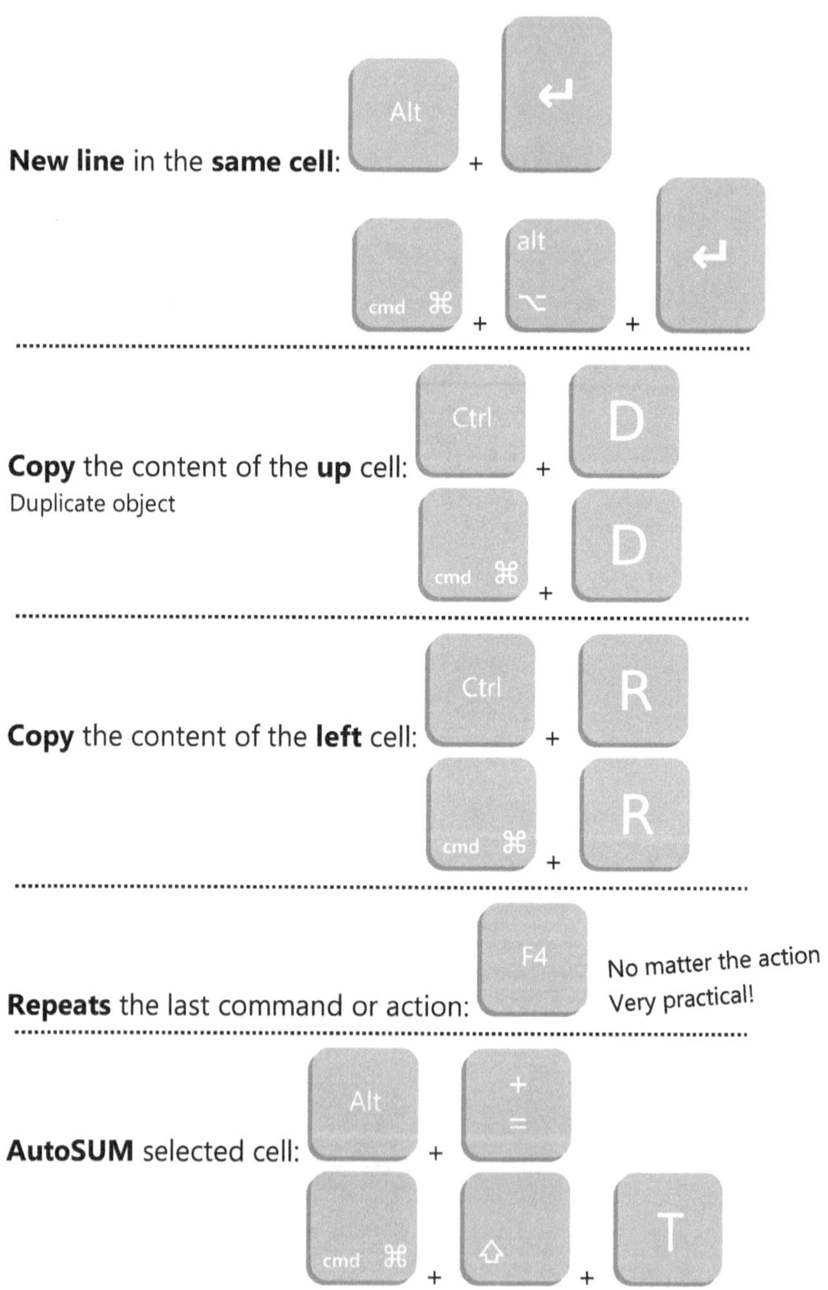

New line in the **same cell**:

Copy the content of the **up** cell:
Duplicate object

Copy the content of the **left** cell:

Repeats the last command or action:
No matter the action
Very practical!

AutoSUM selected cell:

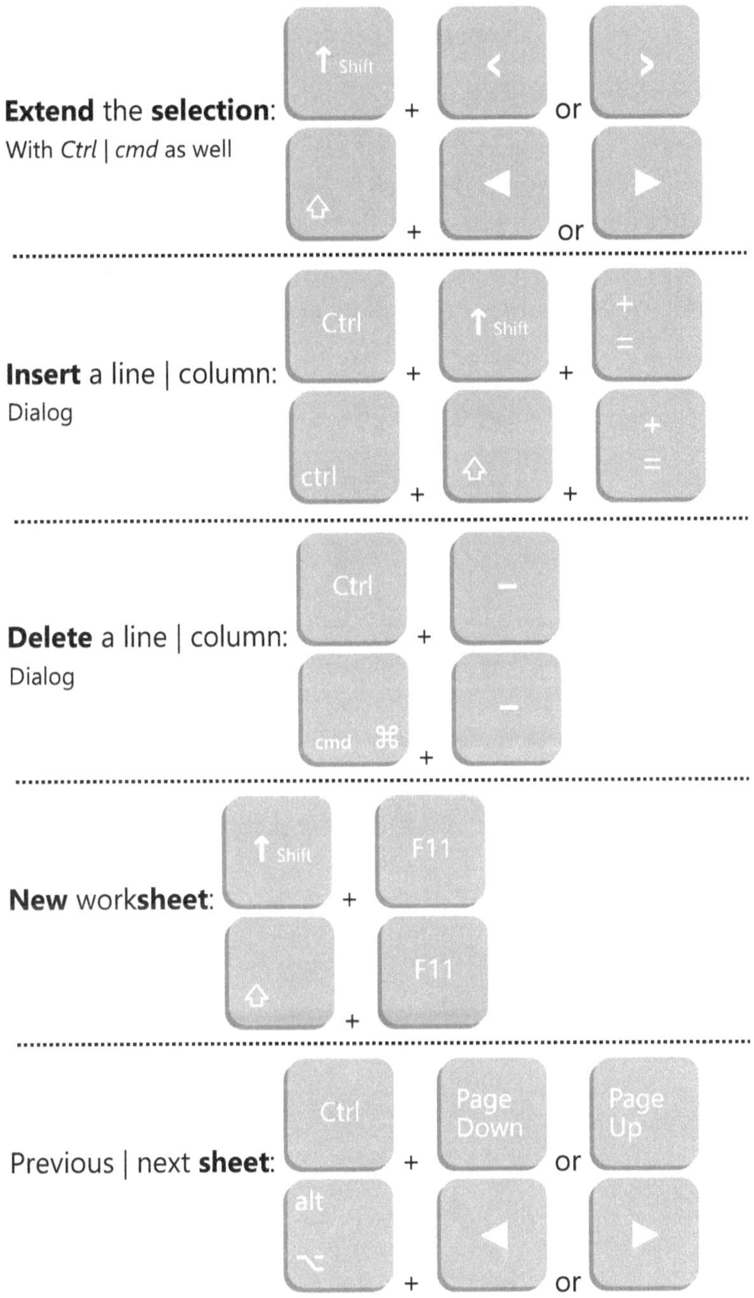

Extend the **selection**:
With *Ctrl* | *cmd* as well

Insert a line | column:
Dialog

Delete a line | column:
Dialog

New work**sheet**:

Previous | next **sheet**:

PowerPoint | .pptx

Except for a few nuances, the keyboard shortcuts in this part will be able to be used on **Libre Office Impress**. To make a **slide**, these software are essential because they are **accessible** and allow you to easily create a **quality project**. In order to better control the multiple accessibility of these software, I will present you their key keyboard shortcuts.

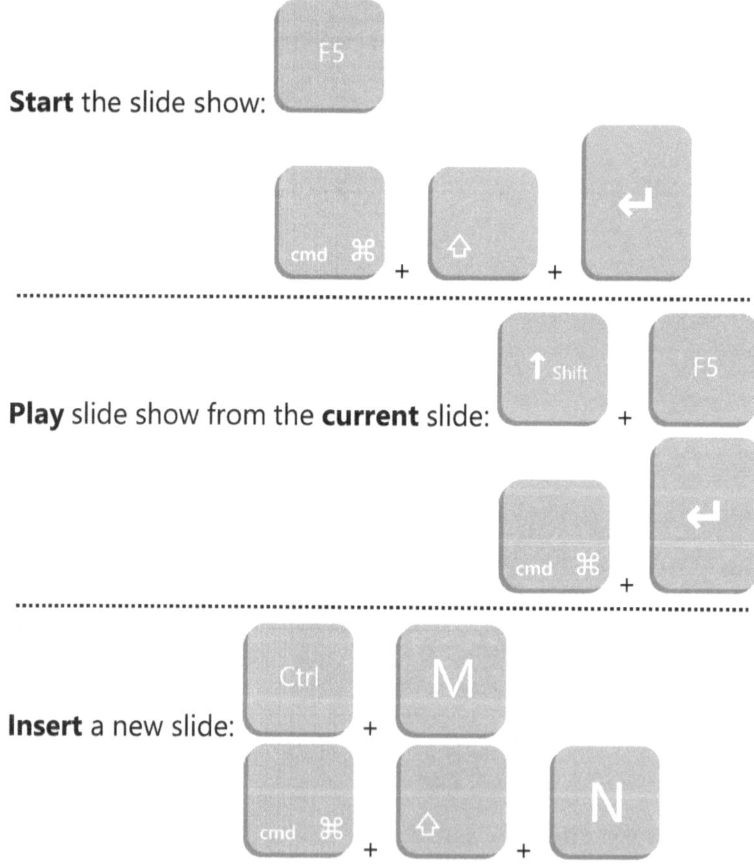

Start the slide show:

Play slide show from the **current** slide:

Insert a new slide:

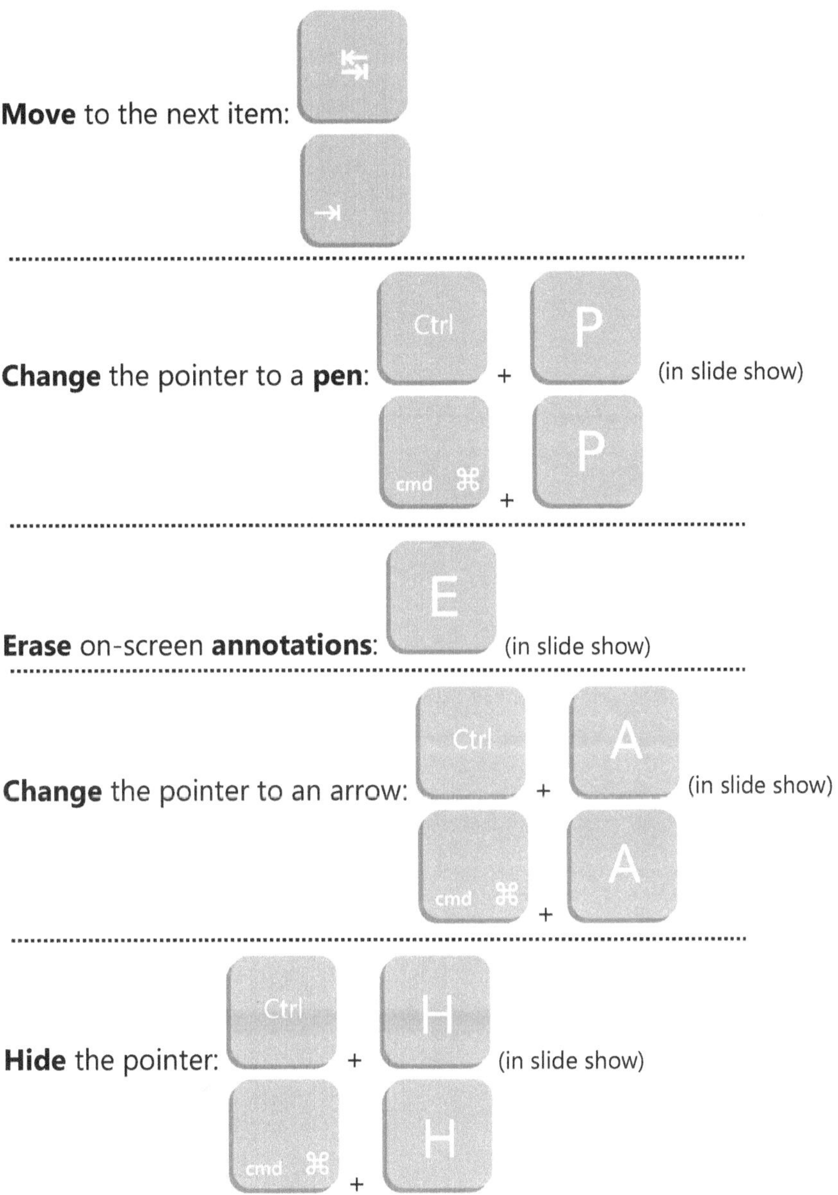

Move to the next item:
Change the pointer to a pen:
Ctrl
P
(in slide show)
cmd
P
Erase on-screen annotations:
E
(in slide show)
Change the pointer to an arrow:
Ctrl
A
(in slide show)
cmd
A
Hide the pointer:
Ctrl
H
(in slide show)
cmd
H

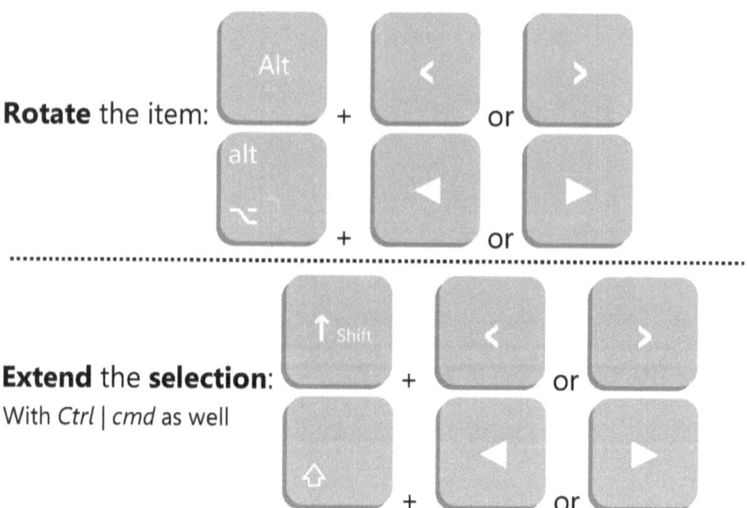

Rotate the item:

Extend the **selection**:
With *Ctrl | cmd* as well

Web Browsers

Google Chrome | Edge | Mozilla Firefox | Brave | Opera

On these web browsers, the keyboard shortcuts remain for the most part **the same**. They are very interesting to master in order to **surf** the web at your own pace.

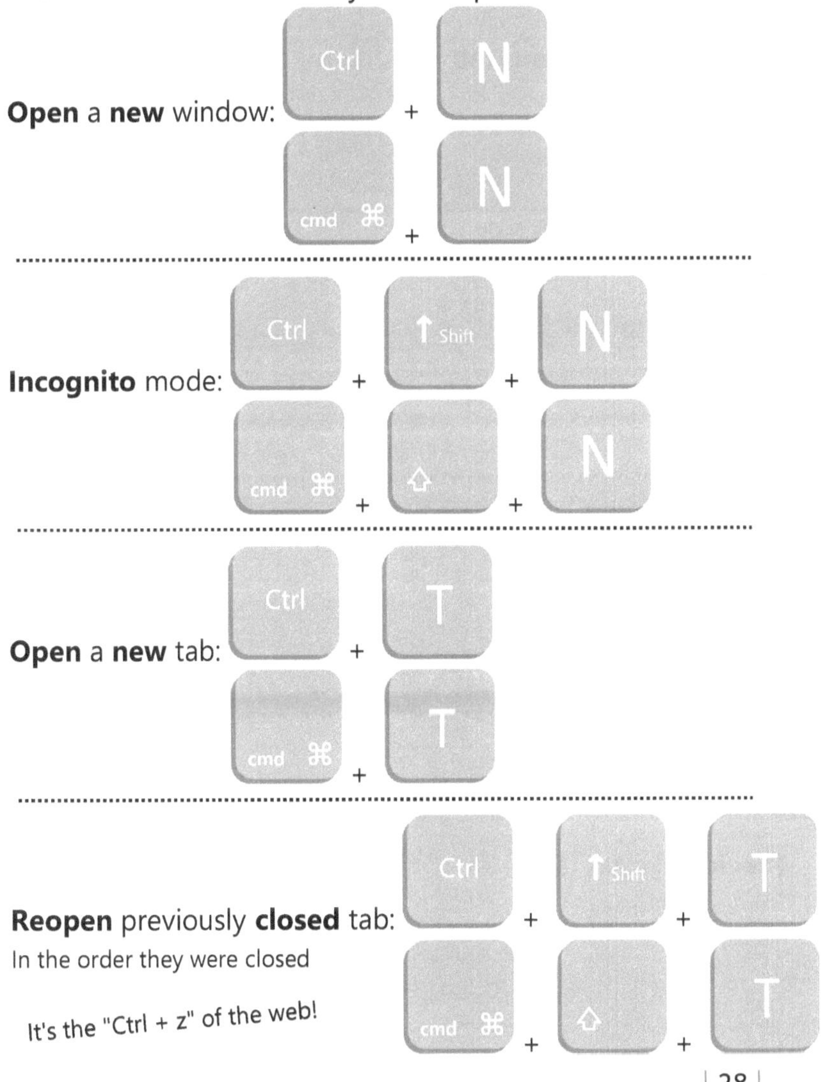

Move to the **next** tab:

Move to the **previous** tab:

The **first 8** tabs:

Last tab:
The
rightmost
tab

Previous | next tab:
From your browsing
history

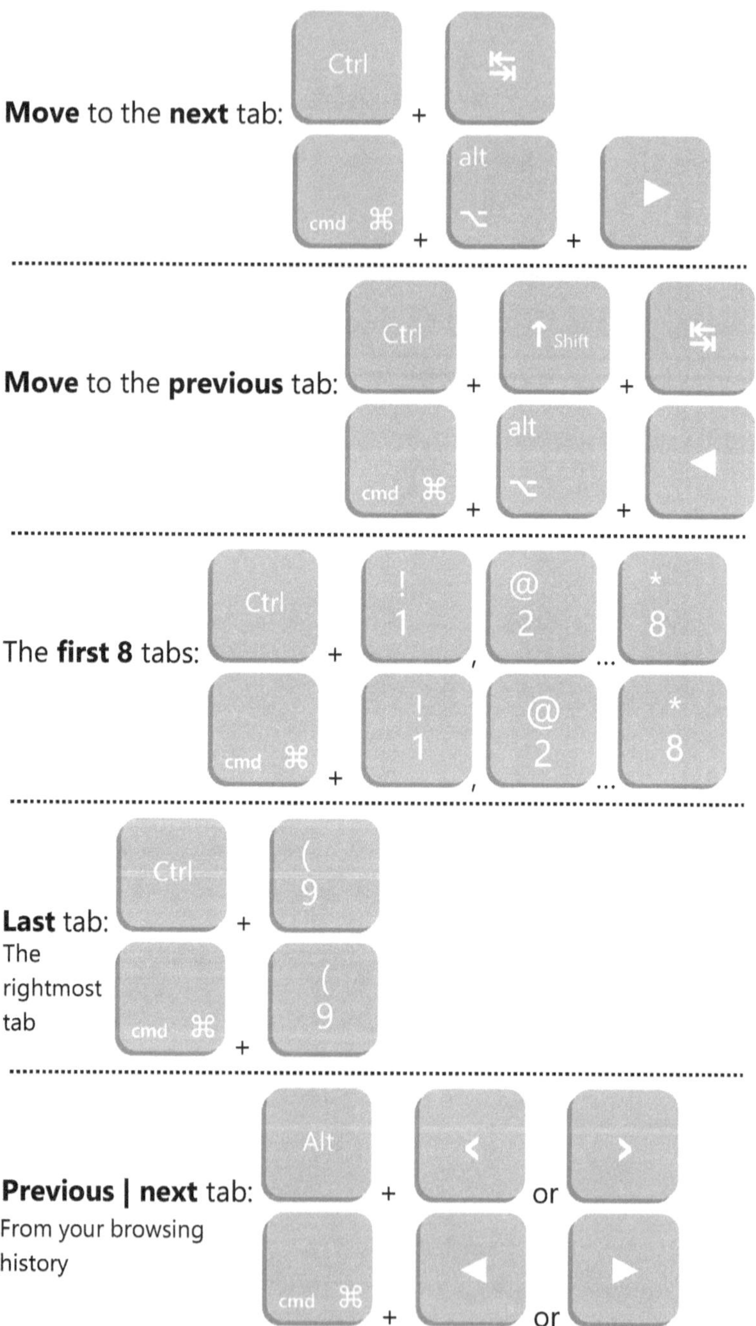

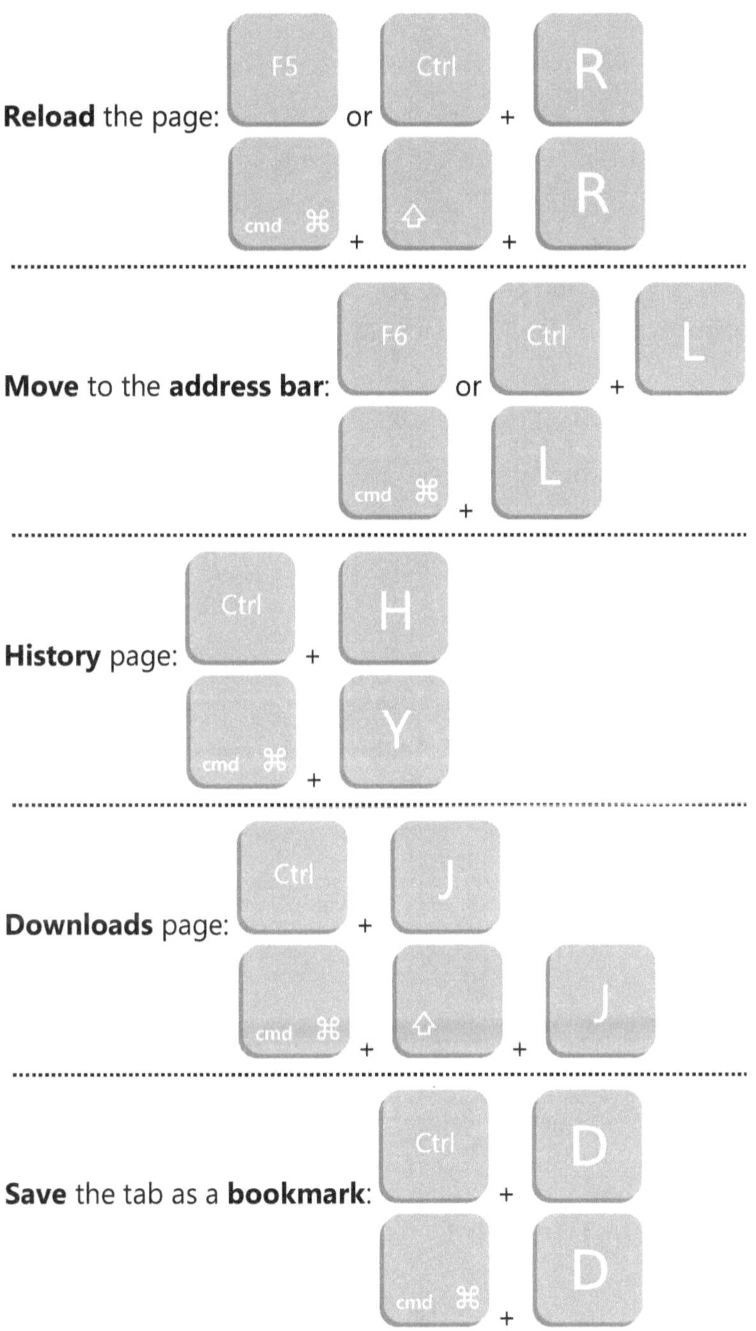

Reload the page: F5 or Ctrl + R
cmd ⌘ + ⇧ + R

Move to the address bar: F6 or Ctrl + L
cmd ⌘ + L

History page: Ctrl + H
cmd ⌘ + Y

Downloads page: Ctrl + J
cmd ⌘ + ⇧ + J

Save the tab as a bookmark: Ctrl + D
cmd ⌘ + D

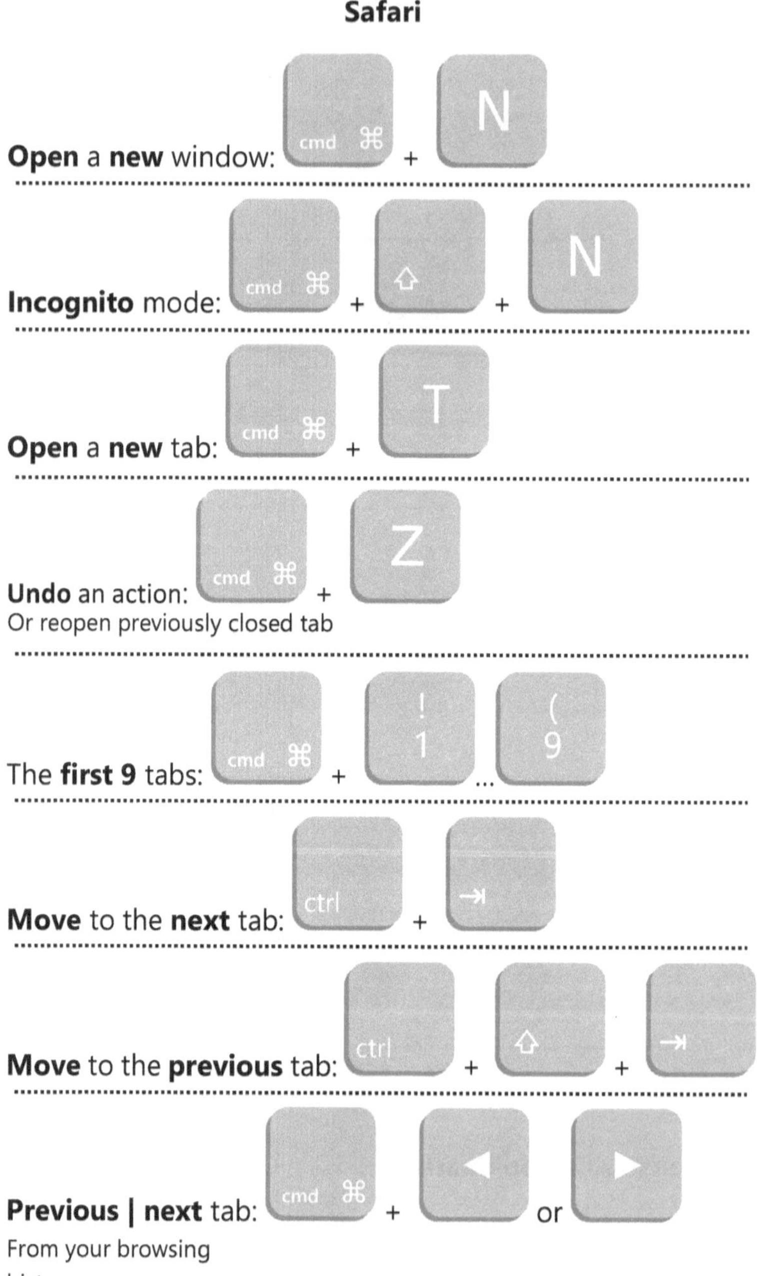

Safari
Open a new window: cmd ⌘ + N
Incognito mode: cmd ⌘ + ⇧ + N
Open a new tab: cmd ⌘ + T
Undo an action: cmd ⌘ + Z
Or reopen previously closed tab
The first 9 tabs: cmd ⌘ + 1 ... 9
Move to the next tab: ctrl + →|
Move to the previous tab: ctrl + ⇧ + →|
Previous | next tab: cmd ⌘ + ◀ or ▶
From your browsing
history

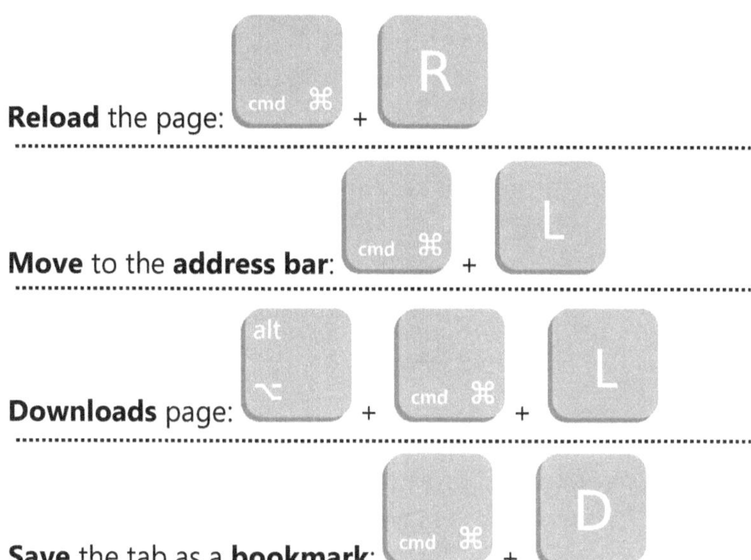

Reload the page: cmd ⌘ + R

Move to the **address bar**:   cmd ⌘ + L

Downloads page: alt + cmd ⌘ + L

Save the tab as a **bookmark**:   cmd ⌘ + D

Google Drive

It is a **Cloud storage solution**, the data is accessible **on all media** (Computers, phones, tablets). It also provides qualitative and professional **tools** very similar to the Microsoft Office suite.

For those who **are not familiar** with these tools, I present you the positive and negative points of these tools:

✓ *Pros*: Saves are **automatic on the Cloud** | The history of previous **versions** and **modifications** are accessible at any time | **Group work** is made easier; it is very simple to work simultaneously on the same document with several people | Each account has a free **15GB** storage space | The tools have **new** functionalities

✗ *Cons*: Functionalities are **limited** compared to the Microsoft Office suite | An **internet connection** is required to save the documents (possibility to access the documents offline)

Here are some keyboard shortcuts for these handy Google applications:

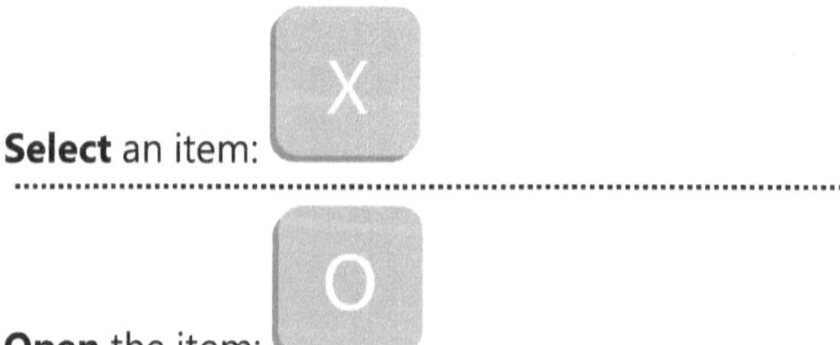

Select an item:

Open the item:

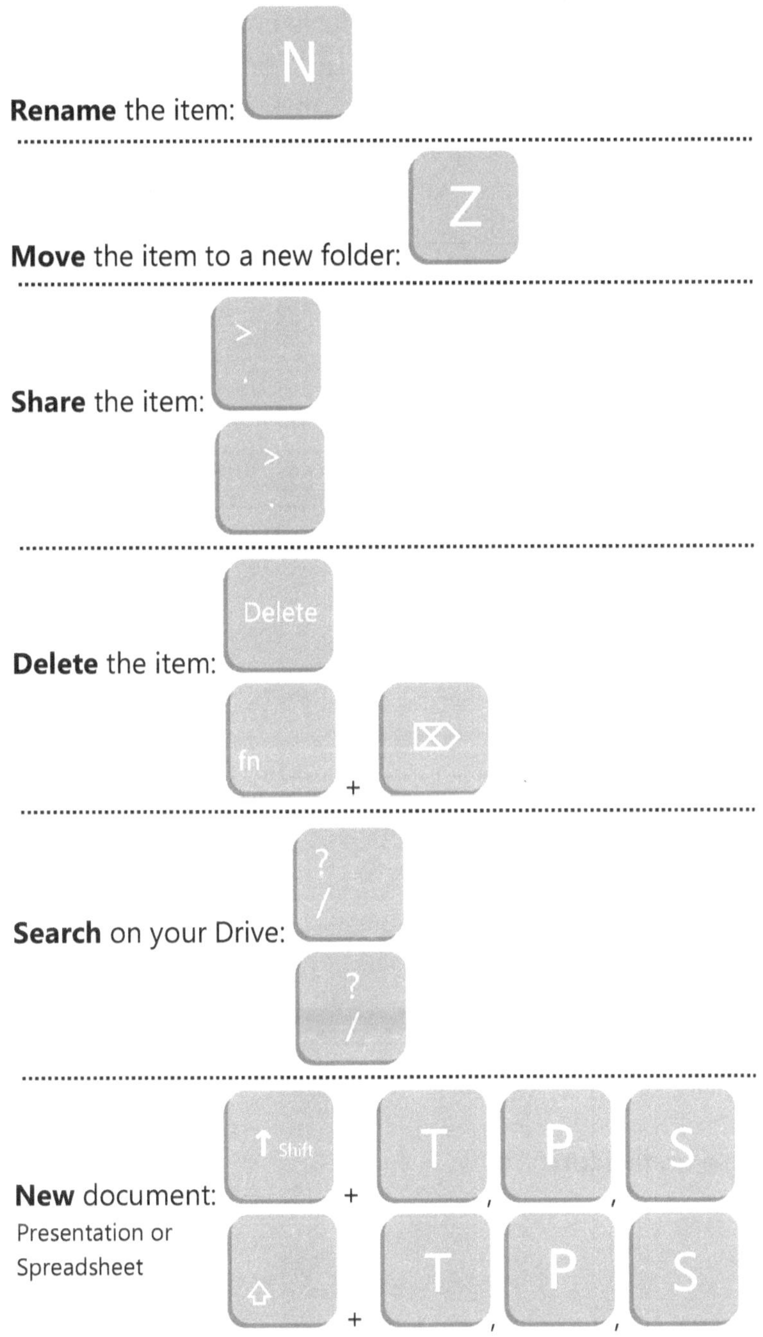

Rename the item:

Move the item to a new folder:

Share the item:

Delete the item:

Search on your Drive:

New document:
Presentation or
Spreadsheet

The **following 3 applications** available on Google Drive for word processing, spreadsheet and presentation have keyboard shortcuts **in common**. Some general keyboard shortcuts at the beginning of the book may apply.

Save: automatic!

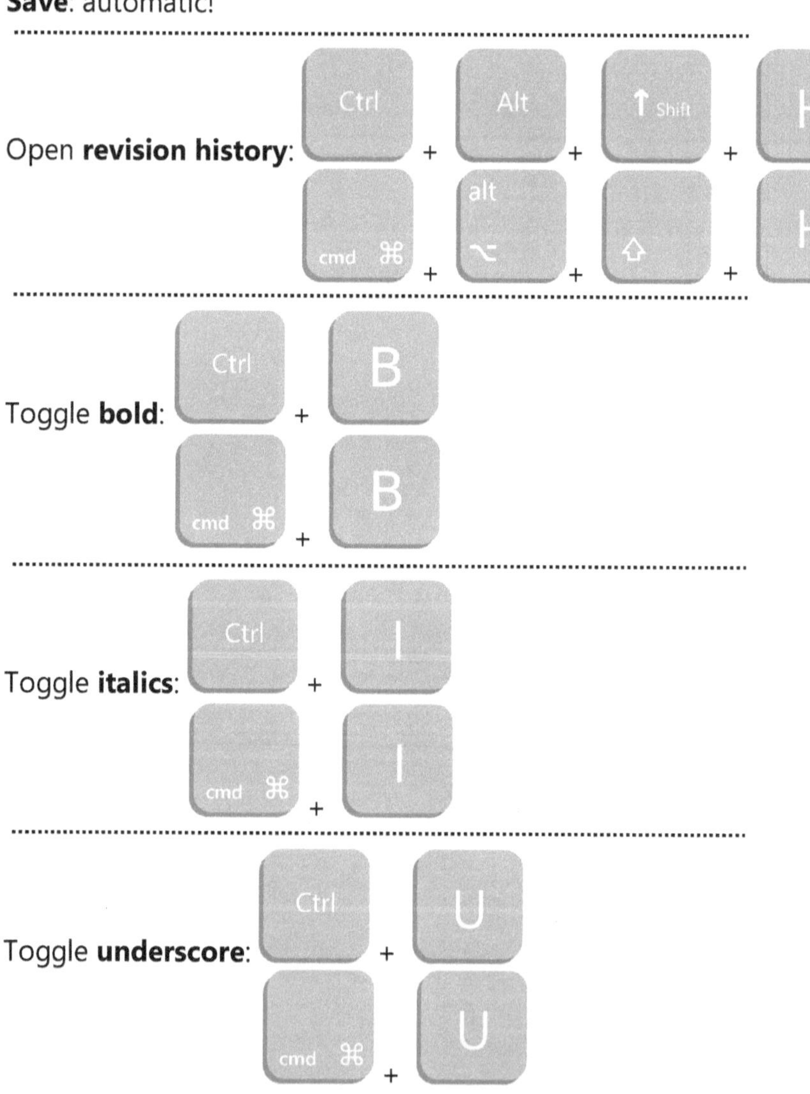

Open **revision history**:

Toggle **bold**:

Toggle **italics**:

Toggle **underscore**:

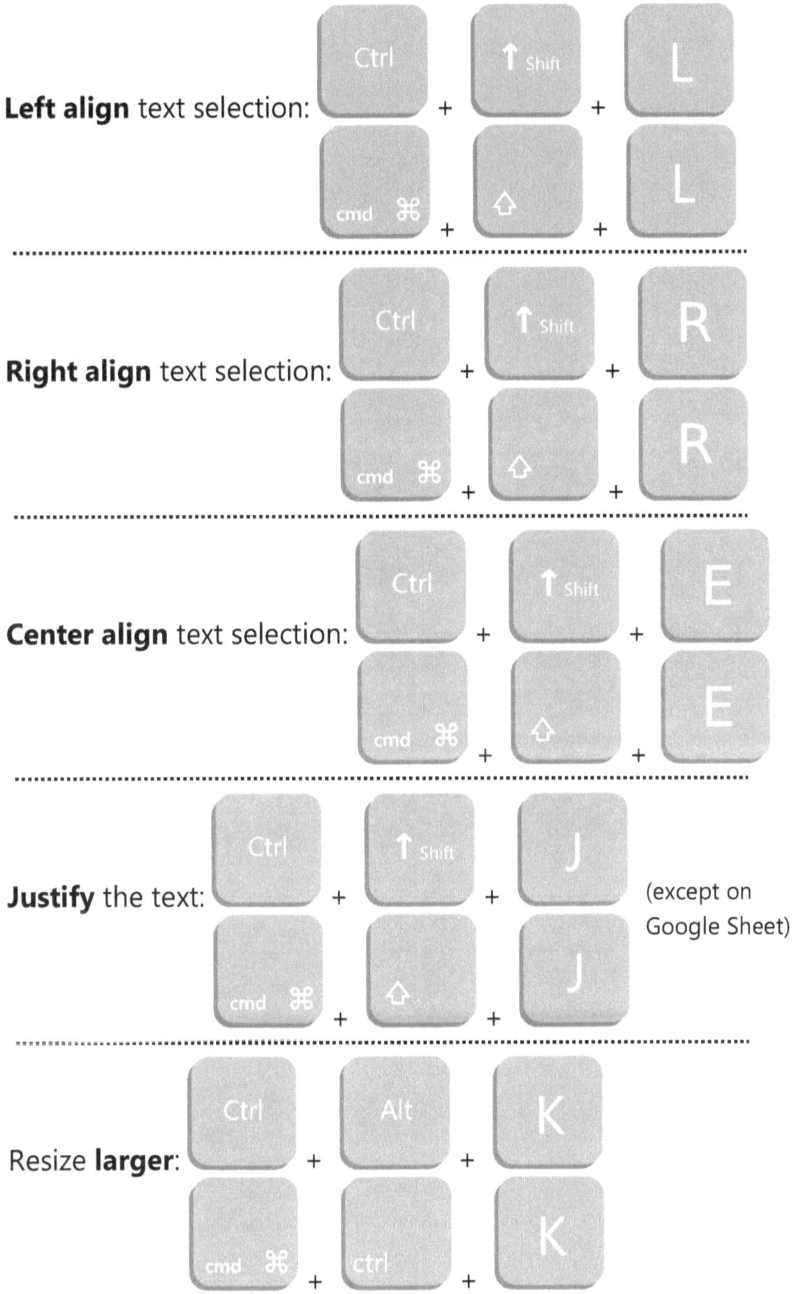

Left align text selection:
Ctrl + ↑ Shift + L
cmd ⌘ + ⇧ + L

Right align text selection:
Ctrl + ↑ Shift + R
cmd ⌘ + ⇧ + R

Center align text selection:
Ctrl + ↑ Shift + E
cmd ⌘ + ⇧ + E

Justify the text:
Ctrl + ↑ Shift + J
cmd ⌘ + ⇧ + J
(except on Google Sheet)

Resize larger:
Ctrl + Alt + K
cmd ⌘ + ctrl + K

Resize **smaller**:
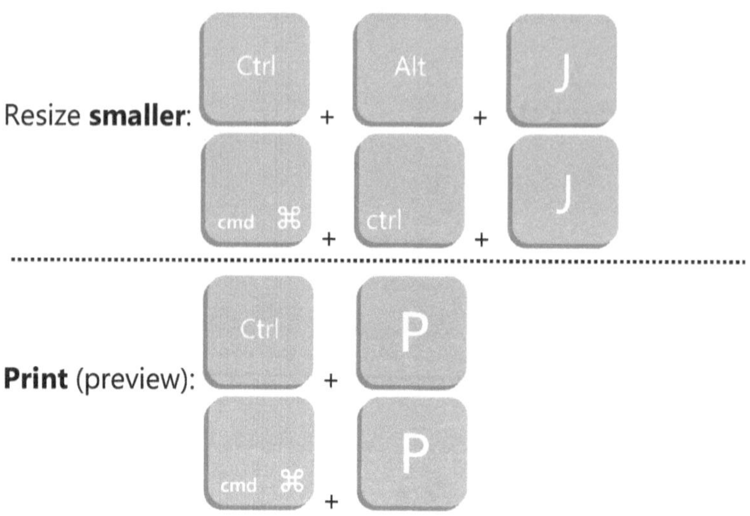

Print (preview):

Google Docs

This application from Google is the same as **Word** or **Open Office Writer**.

Increase font size:
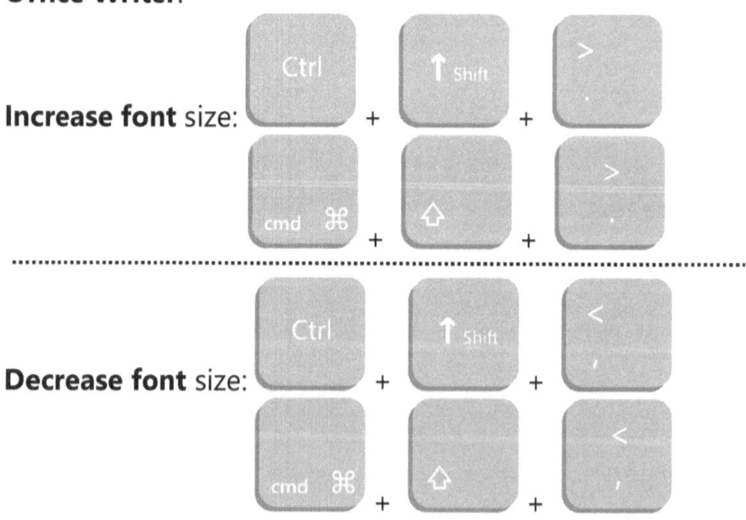

Decrease font size:

Insert a page **break**:

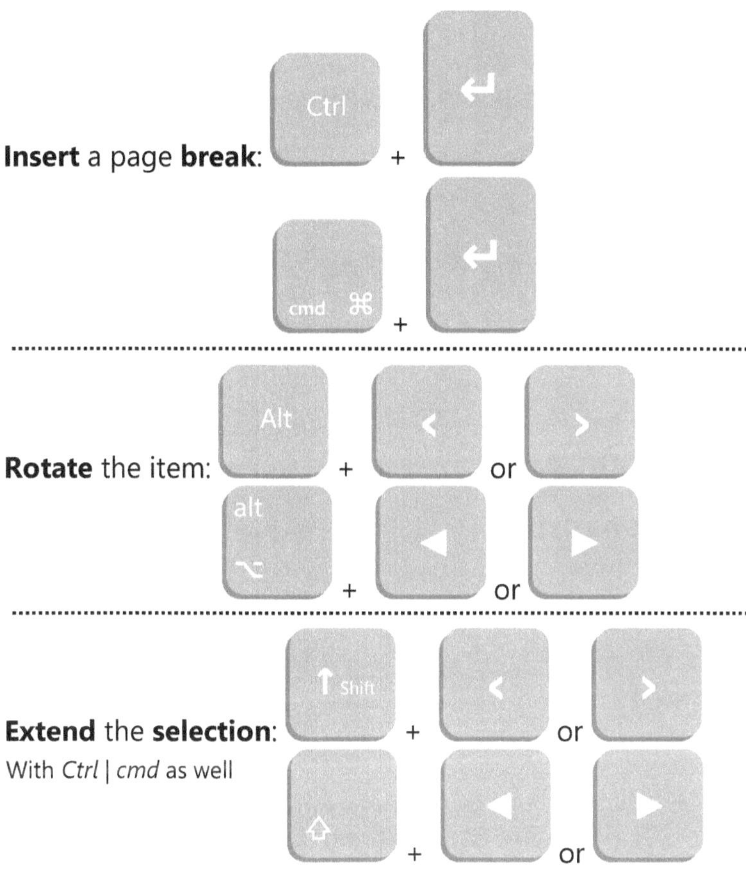

Rotate the item:

Extend the **selection**:
With *Ctrl | cmd* as well

Google Sheets

This is the Google application which can be similar to **Excel** or **Open Office Calc**.

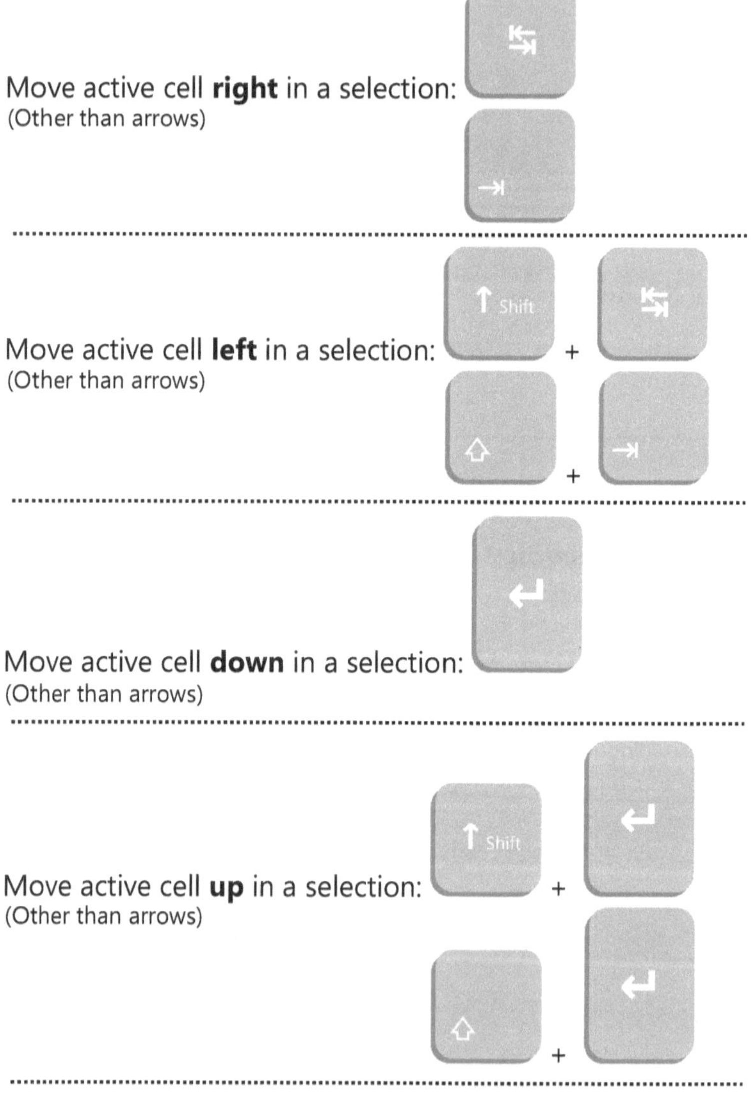

Move active cell **right** in a selection:
(Other than arrows)

Move active cell **left** in a selection:
(Other than arrows)

Move active cell **down** in a selection:
(Other than arrows)

Move active cell **up** in a selection:
(Other than arrows)

Little trick to adjust the **column** or the **line** to the text: double click on the line separating 2 columns or 2 lines when this **arrow** is displayed: ⟷

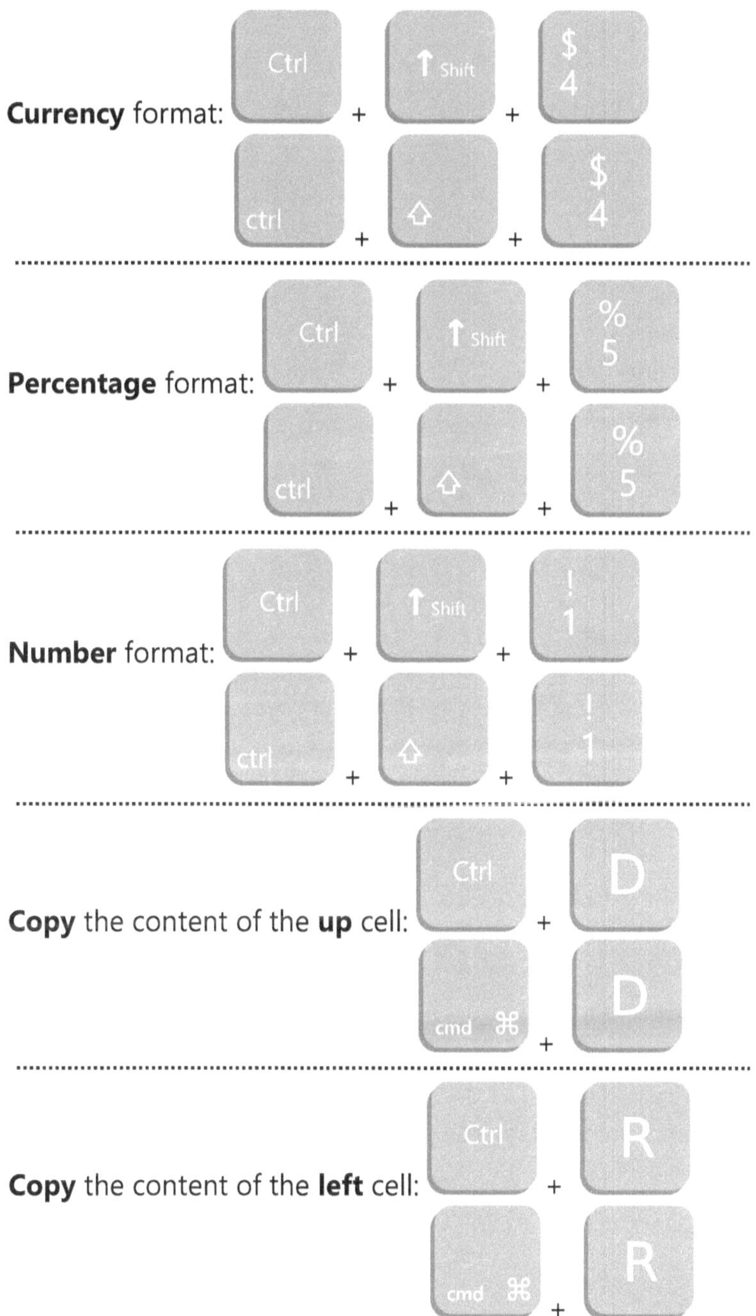

Currency format:
Ctrl + ↑ Shift + $ 4
ctrl + ⇧ + $ 4

Percentage format:
Ctrl + ↑ Shift + % 5
ctrl + ⇧ + % 5

Number format:
Ctrl + ↑ Shift + ! 1
ctrl + ⇧ + ! 1

Copy the content of the up cell:
Ctrl + D
cmd ⌘ + D

Copy the content of the left cell:
Ctrl + R
cmd ⌘ + R

(R | W | B: for a line)
(C | O: for a column)
Insert a line | column:
+ *Maj* (if bug)

(D: for a line)
(E: for a column)
Delete a line | column:
+ *Maj* (if bug)

New work**sheet**:

Previous | next **sheet**:

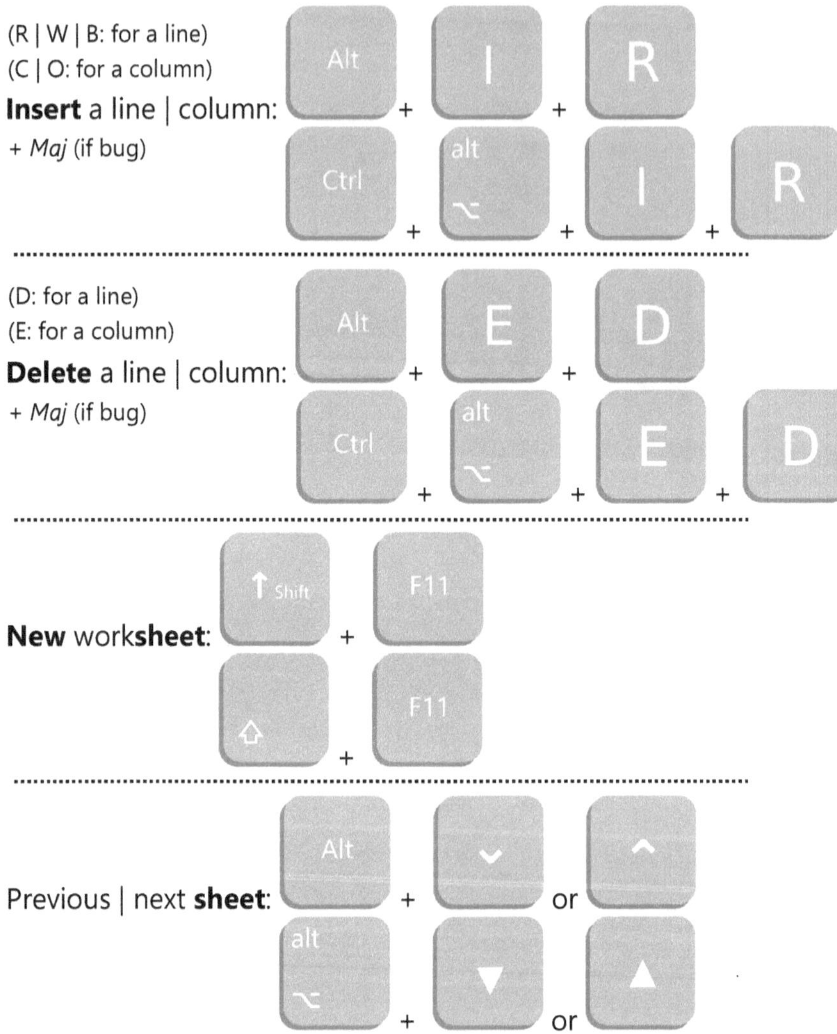

Google Slide

As well as **PowerPoint** or **Open Office Impress**, Google provides a presentation software.

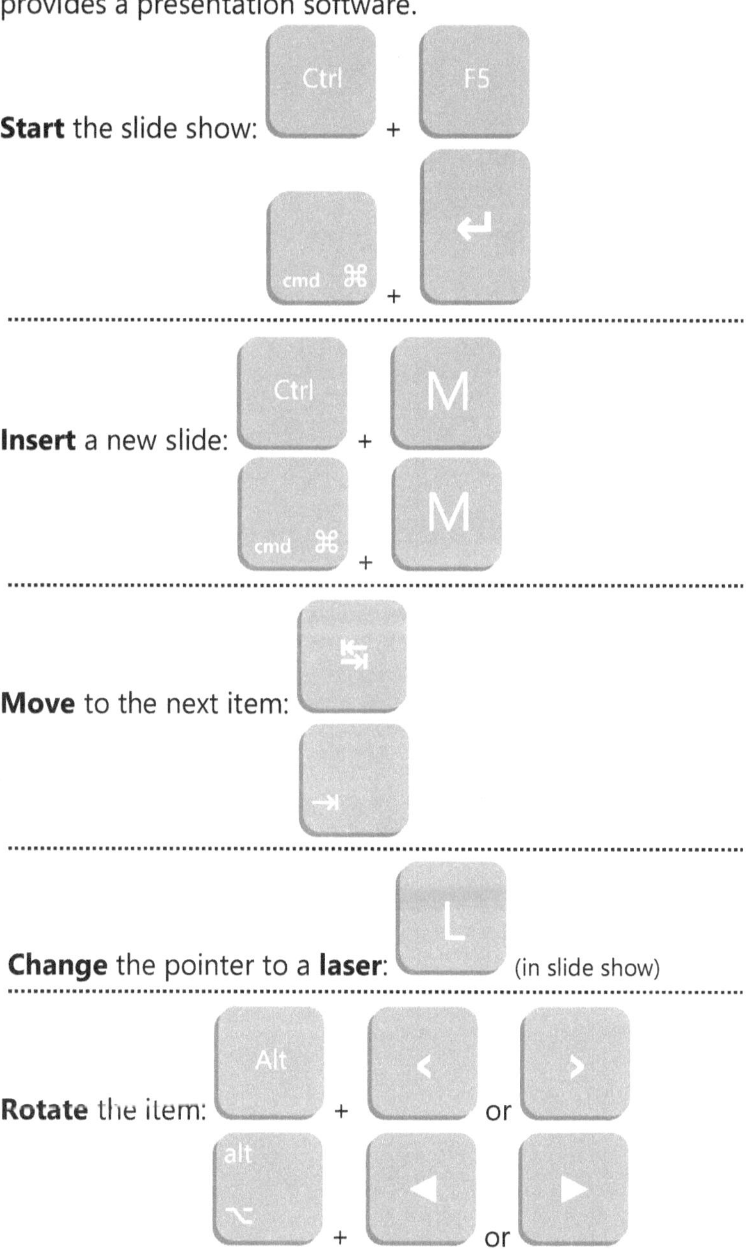

Start the slide show: Ctrl + F5

cmd ⌘ + ↵

Insert a new slide: Ctrl + M

cmd ⌘ + M

Move to the next item: ⇆

⇥

Change the pointer to a **laser**: L (in slide show)

Rotate the item: Alt + < or >

alt ⌥ + ◀ or ▶

Increase font size:

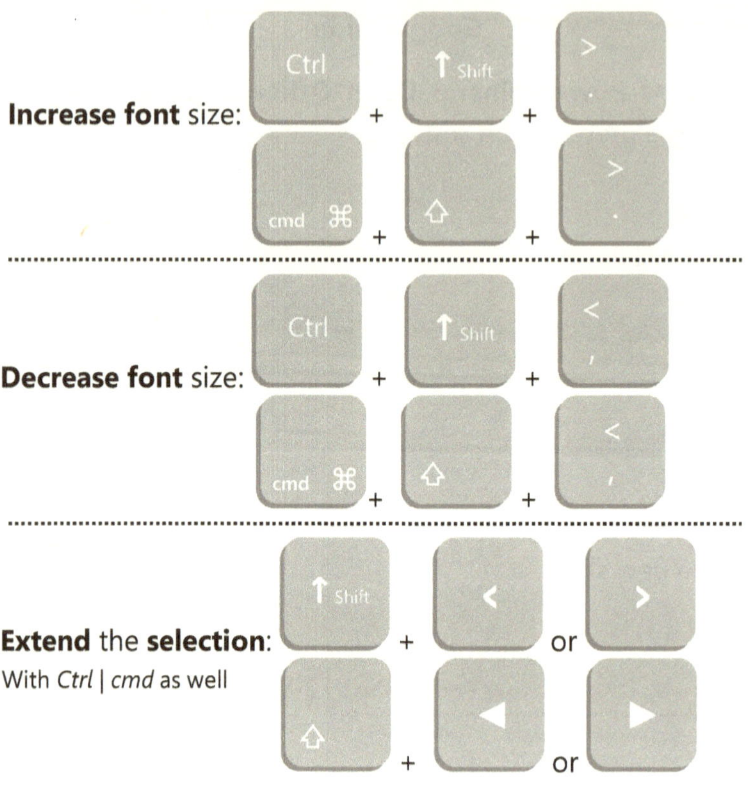

Decrease font size:

Extend the **selection**:
With *Ctrl | cmd* as well

Gmail

For this webmail, which is **very widespread** and **easy to use**, creating an address is extremely simple. Some keyboard shortcuts can be used on this tool. Basic, they do not necessarily work. To **enable** them: Settings → Show all settings → General (scroll down) → Keyboard shortcuts → Enable keyboard shortcuts → Save changes

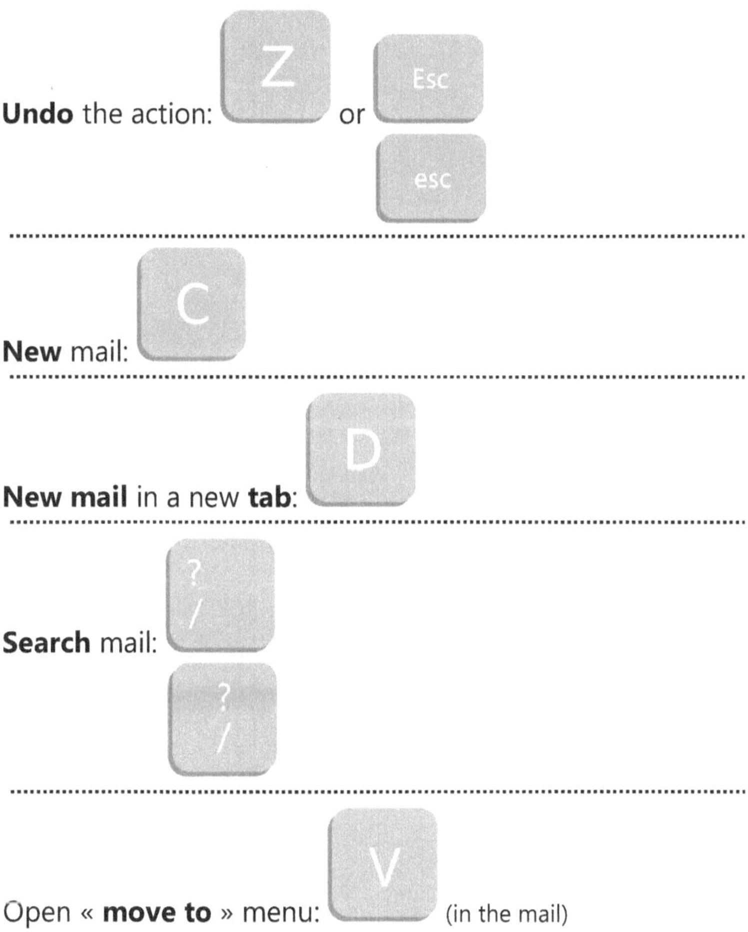

Undo the action: Z or Esc / esc

New mail: C

New mail in a new **tab**: D

Search mail: ? / / ? /

Open « **move to** » menu: V (in the mail)

Open « **more actions** » menu:

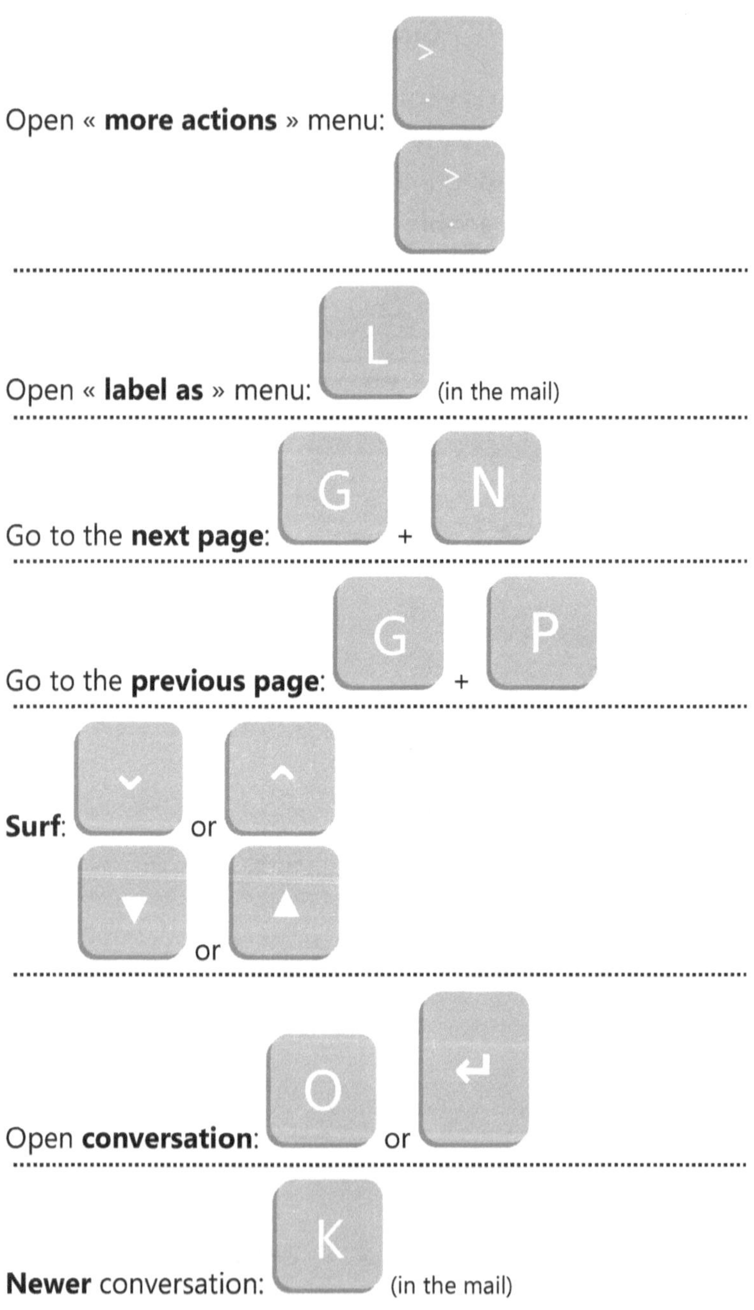

Open « **label as** » menu: (in the mail)

Go to the **next page**: +

Go to the **previous page**: +

Surf: or or

Open **conversation**: or

Newer conversation: (in the mail)

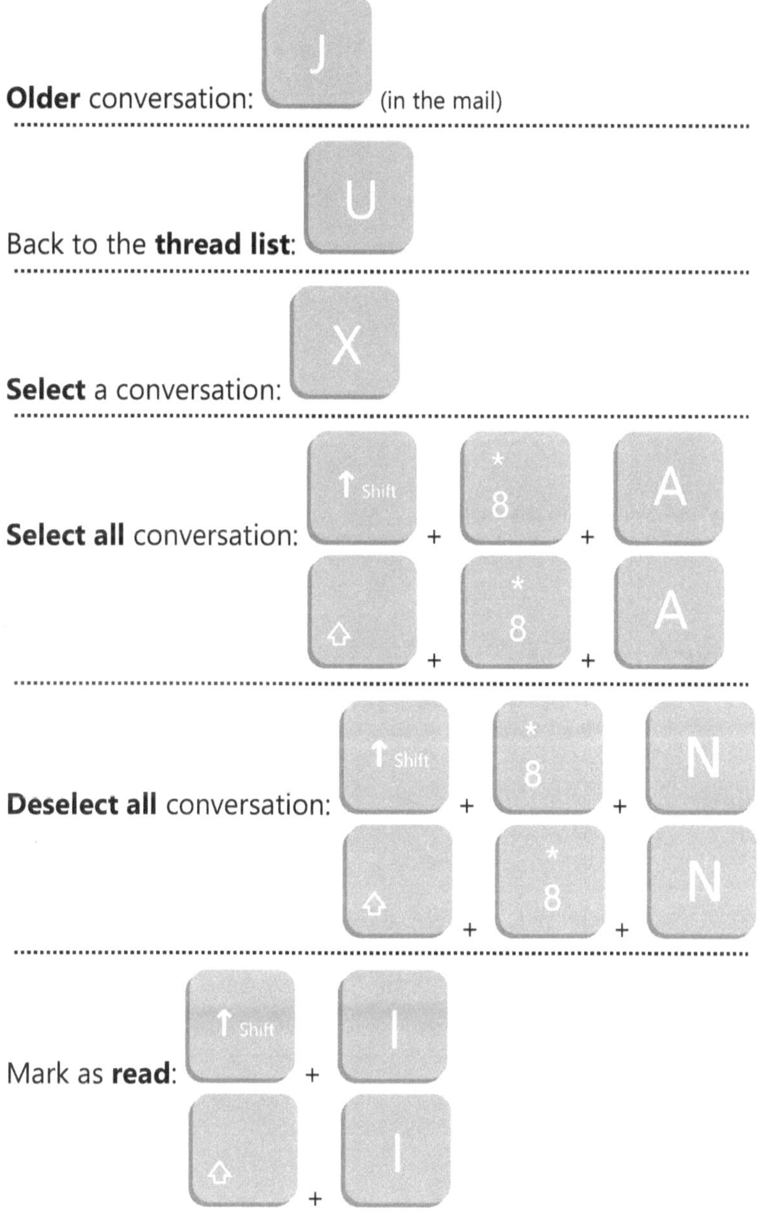

Older conversation: (in the mail)

Back to the **thread list**:

Select a conversation:

Select all conversation:

Deselect all conversation:

Mark as **read**:

Mark as **unread**: 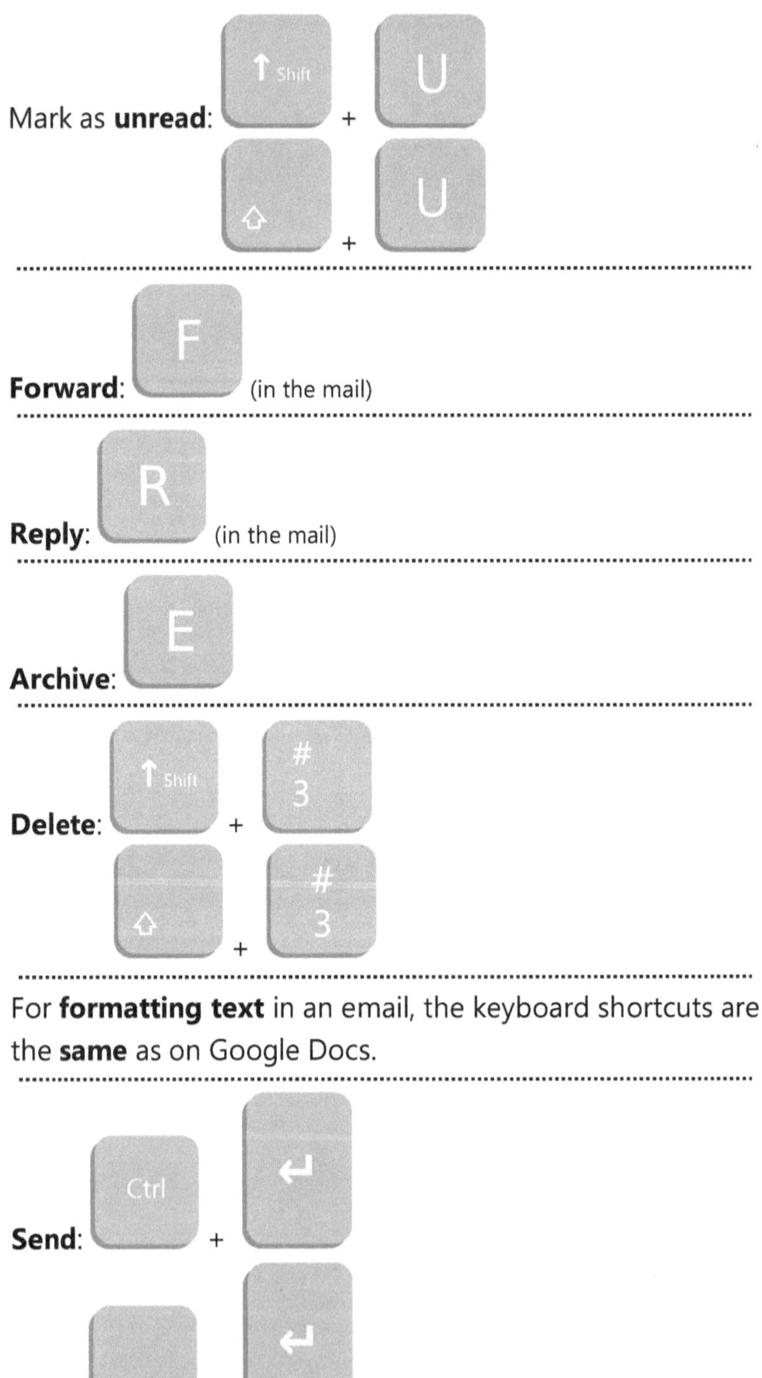

Forward: (in the mail)

Reply: (in the mail)

Archive:

Delete:

For **formatting text** in an email, the keyboard shortcuts are the **same** as on Google Docs.

Send:

Adobe Acrobat Reader DC | PDF | .pdf

Adobe Acrobat Reader DC is the **most famous** software for PDF, it is free for limited use.

A **Portal Document Format** is a type of file and not a software, however, I have included it here since it is frequently used with previous software (exporting a document, web browsers to view ...). A PDF is a **universal** and **standard** file format, it **preserves the presentation** of the document (font, images, layout, design...).

✓*Pros*: It is very easy to **share** | The size of the file is **lighter** than the original | It can be **read on any software/device** (free or not) and therefore on all platforms | It facilitates **printing** conditions (device, quality...) | The file is exported as an "image" (the presentation of the document is fixed)

✗*Cons*: Once the file has been exported as a PDF, it normally remains **unchangeable** (some tools on the web allow you to go backwards) | To modify a PDF (put text, sign, resemble/separate one or several PDF, you have to use a tool: available for free on the web or paying, to have all the functionalities, with Adobe Acrobat Reader DC (with the paying version)).

Keyboard shortcuts are handy when **analyzing** a PDF, but they must be **activated** (if not done in the basic way): Editions → Preferences → General → Use one-touch keys to access the tools (at the very top) → Click on OK

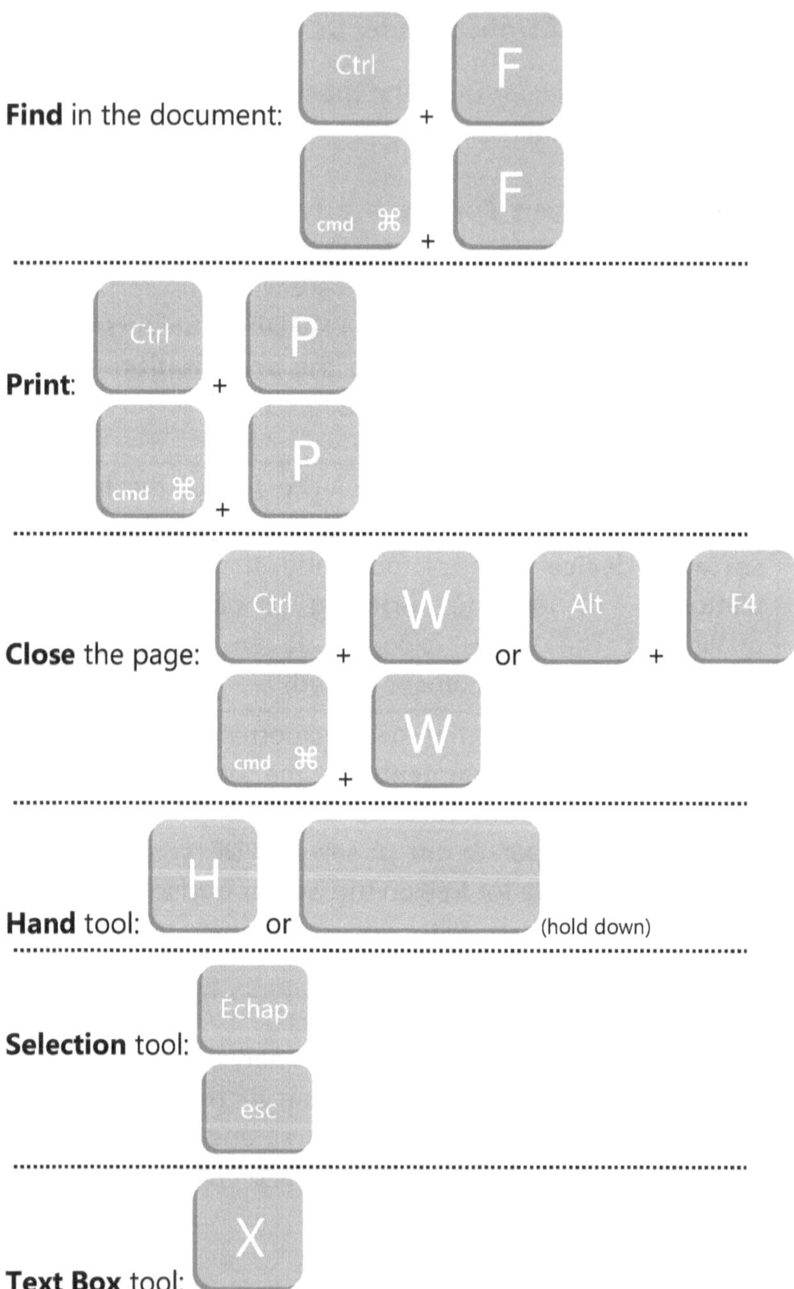

Find in the document:

Print:

Close the page: or

Hand tool: or (hold down)

Selection tool:

Text Box tool:

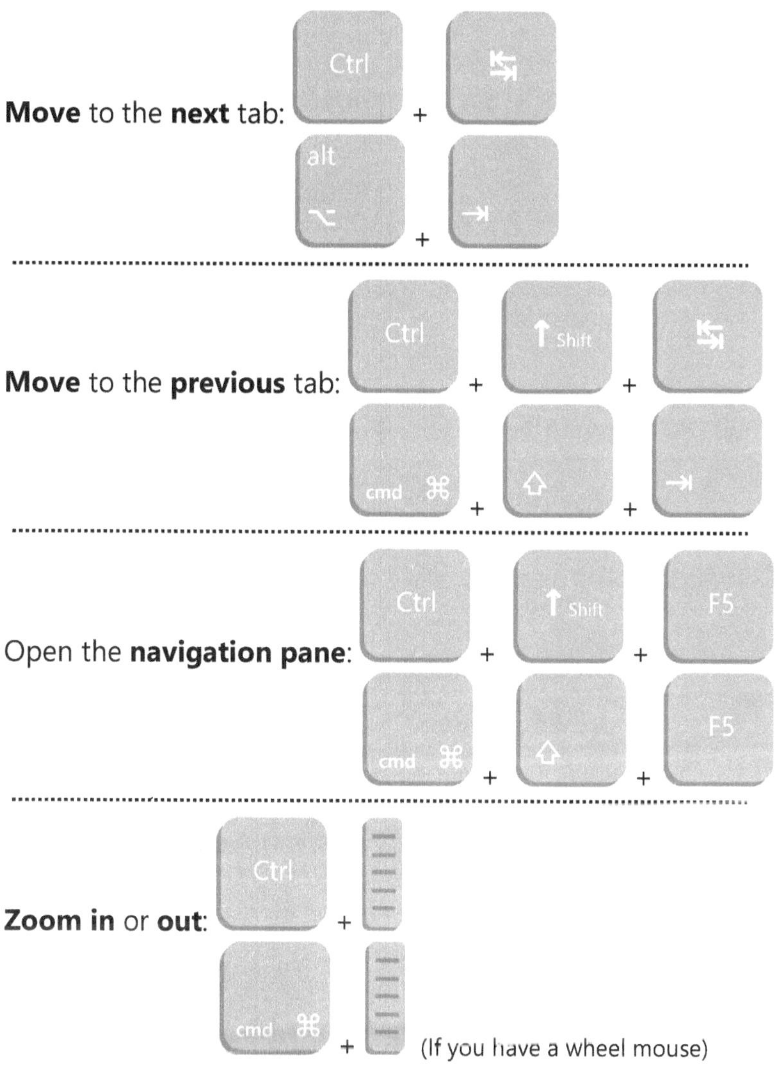

Move to the next tab:
Ctrl
+
+
Move to the previous tab:
Ctrl
Shift
+
+
cmd
+
+
Open the navigation pane:
Ctrl
Shift
F5
+
+
cmd
F5
+
+
Zoom in or out:
Ctrl
+
cmd
+
(If you have a wheel mouse)

YouTube

When searching for **videos** on YouTube, keyboard shortcuts are also useful to get easier access to certain **features**.

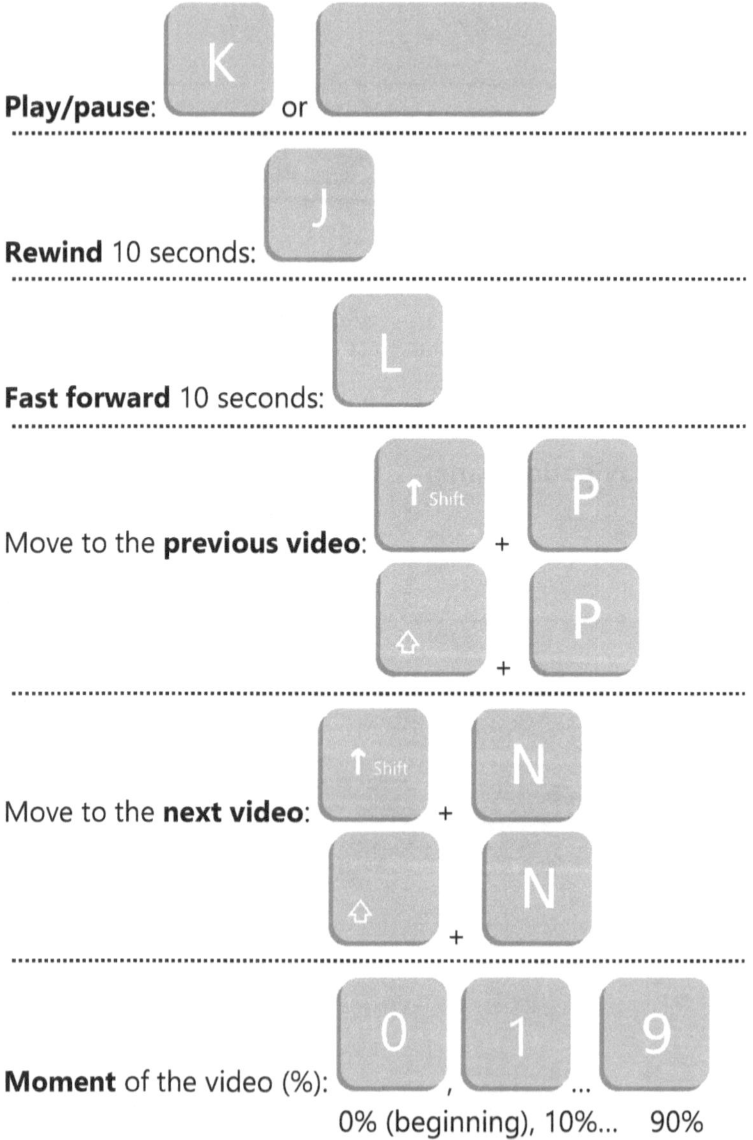

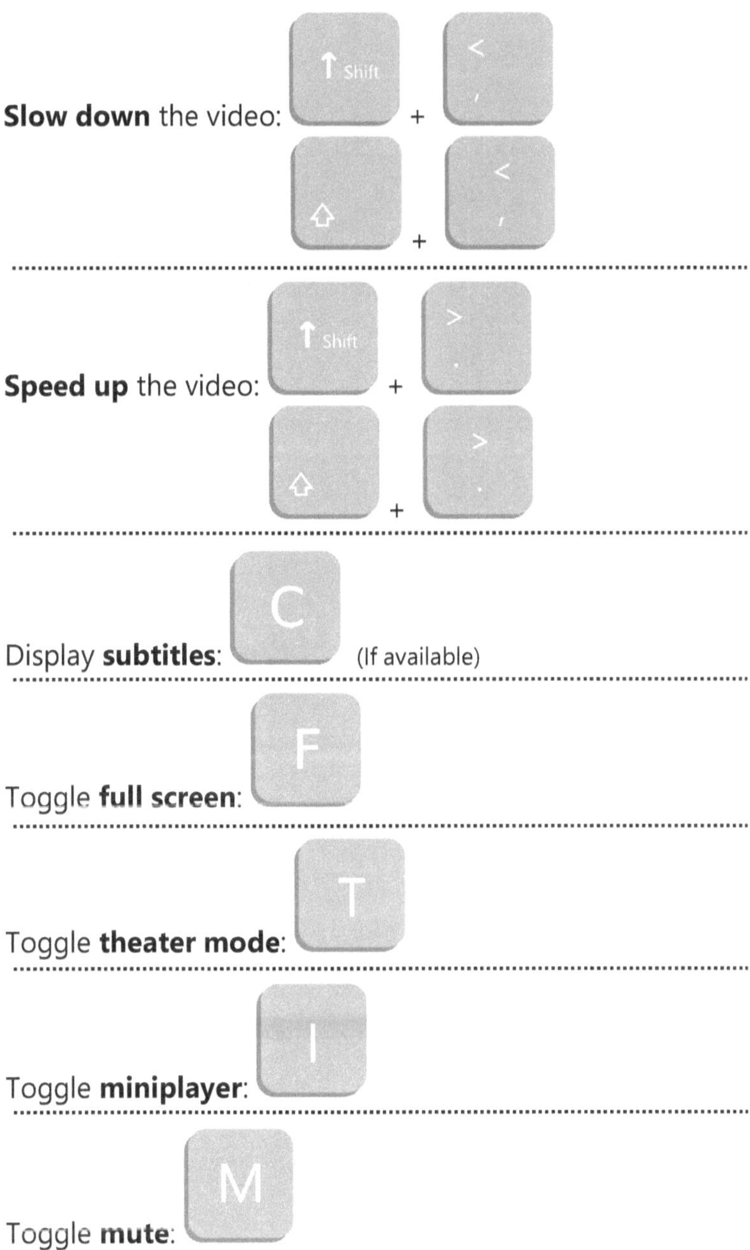

Slow down the video: +

Speed up the video: +

Display **subtitles**:   (If available)

Toggle **full screen**:

Toggle **theater mode**:

Toggle **miniplayer**:

Toggle **mute**:

Decrease volume: 5%

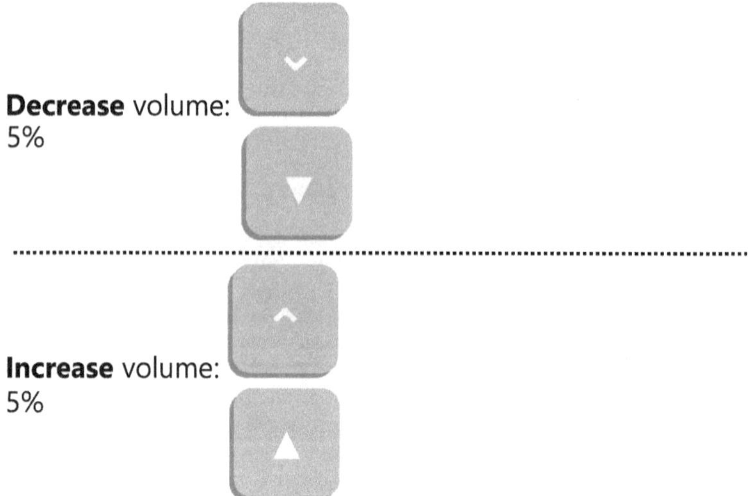

Increase volume: 5%

Touchpad | Trackpad | Pad

If you don't have a mouse, the touchpad replaces the mouse while still enjoying some **advantages** over laptops. It is interesting to know the different possibilities that the Touchpad/Trackpad can offer by using gestures with **several fingers**, even if the mouse remains the favorite with its precision, ergonomics and simplicity.

Windows 10:

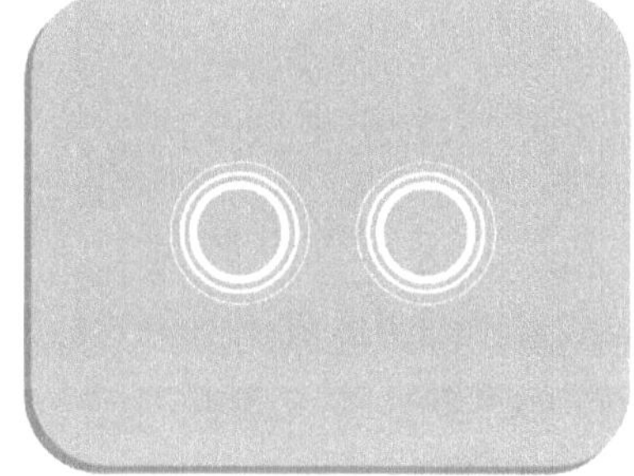

Right click (as on the mouse):

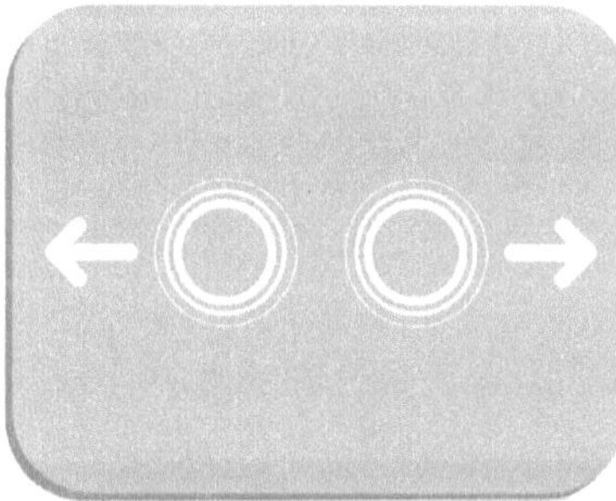

: **Zoom in**

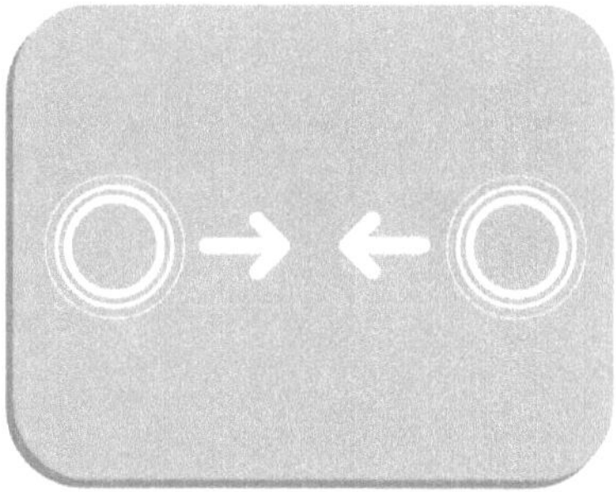

Zoom out:

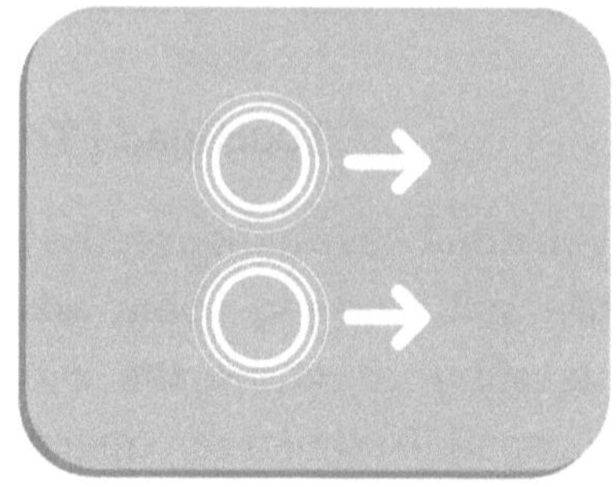

Scroll **horizontally**, left or right (on PDF, pages...):

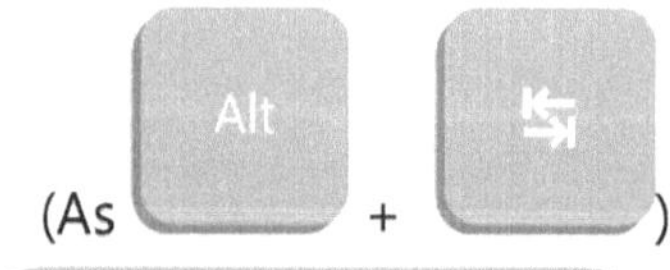

: Scroll **vertically**, up or down (on PDF, web browsers...)

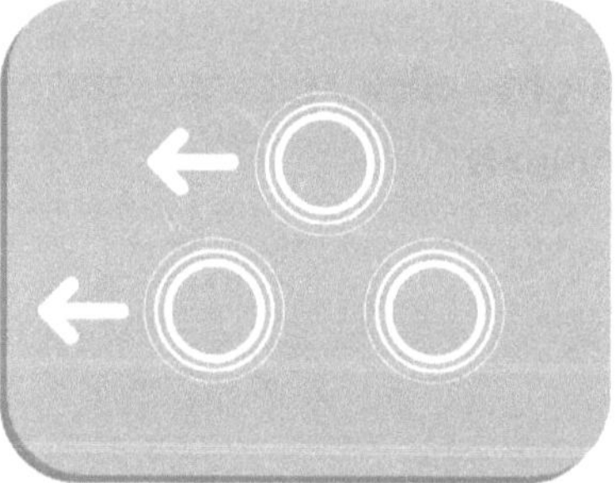

Navigate between several **windows**, to the left or to the right:

(As [Alt] + [⇆])

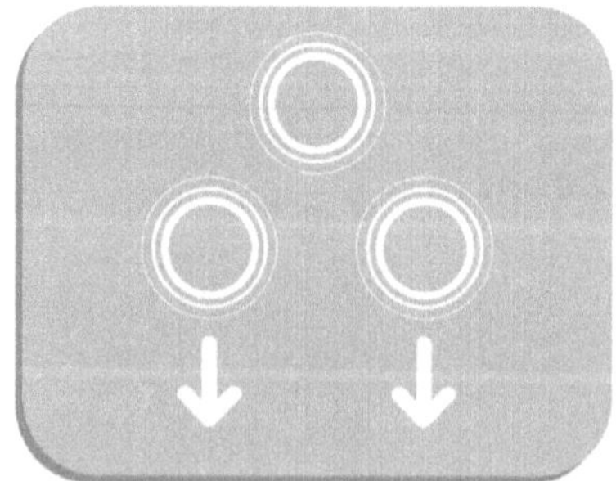

: Display the **desktop**, or move up the 3 fingers to enlarge the window

(As [⊞] + [D])

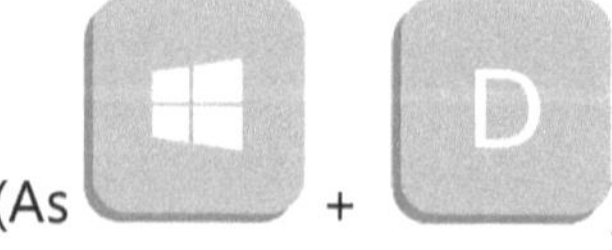

These gestures can be **changed** in the Menu → System Preferences → Trackpad

Right click (as on the mouse)
Double tap to zoom in or out with **Smart zoom**:

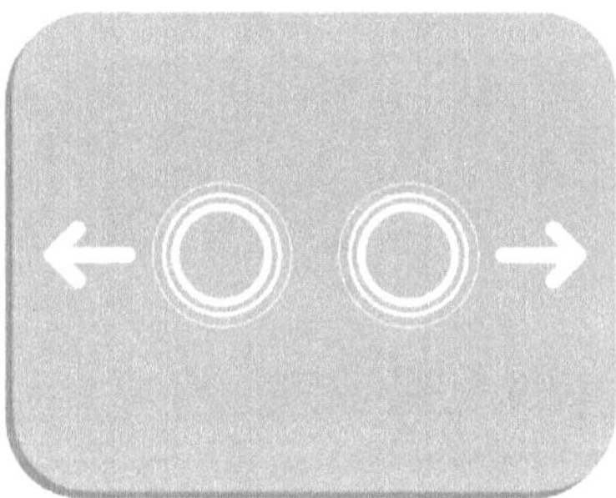

: **Zoom in**

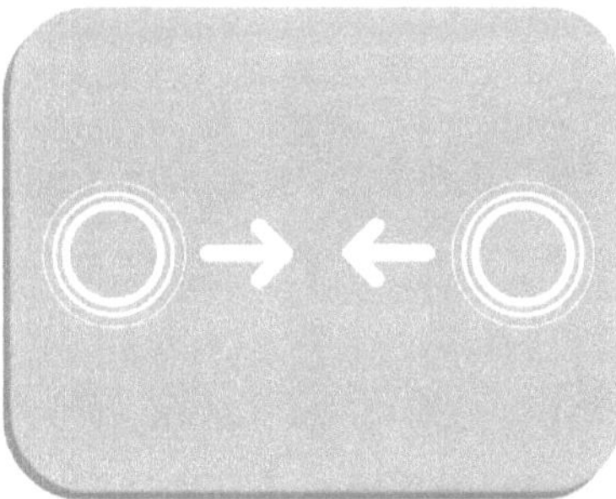

Zoom out:

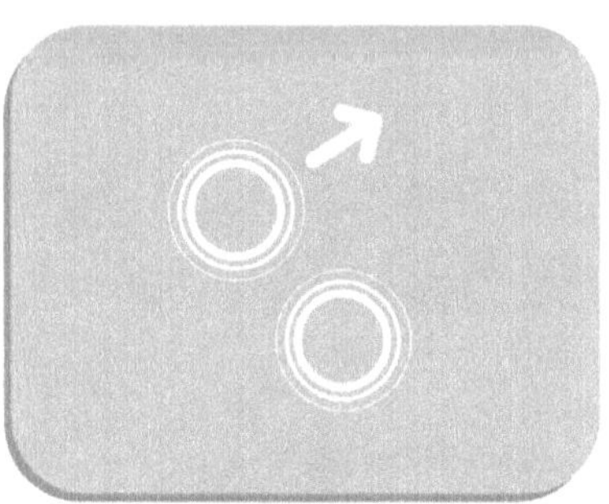

: **Rotating** the element to the right or left

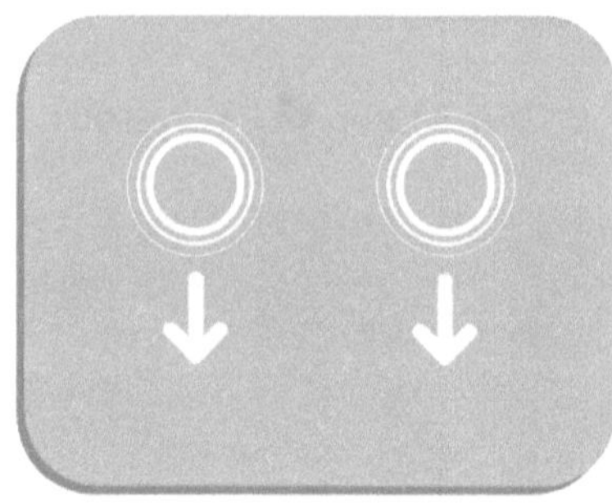

As the mouse wheel

: Scroll **vertically**, up or down (on PDF, web browsers...)

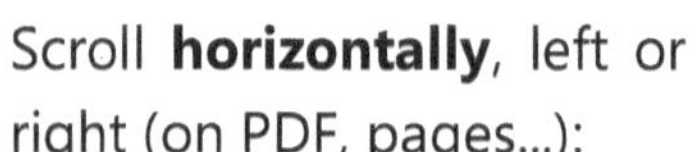

Scroll **horizontally**, left or right (on PDF, pages...):

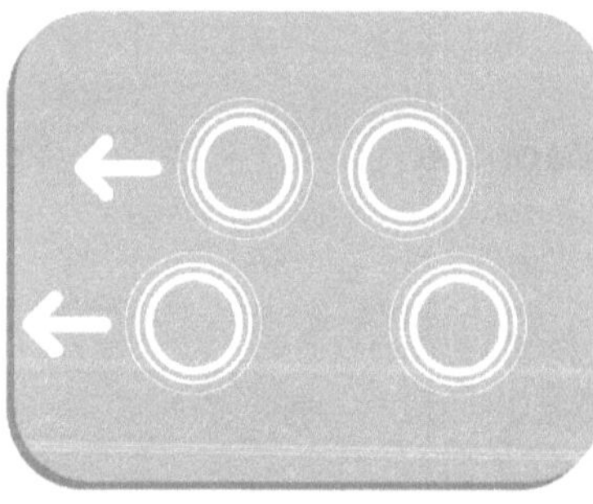

: Navigate between several **windows**, to the left or to the right

(As 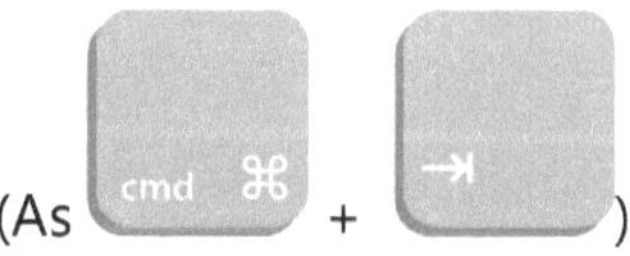 +)

Display the **desktop**, or move up the 3 fingers to enlarge the window:

(As 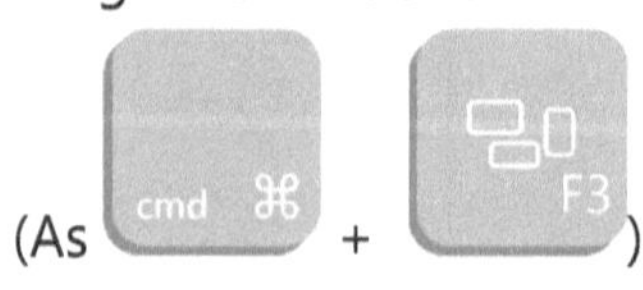 +)

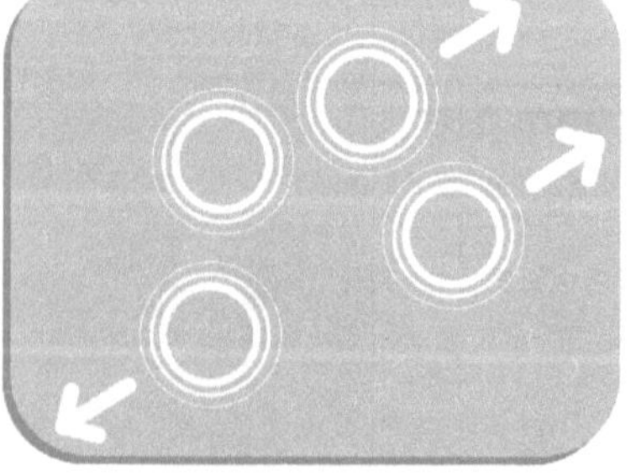

It takes some **agility**, good **training**!

Image | .png | .jpeg

There are several **image formats** that have their own specificities. In order to understand their differences, I will stay in the generality and show you the main types of formats you will encounter most frequently for a **common** use. (On the web and image processing)

PNG | .png	This format is called Portal Network Graphics, and is one of the most widely used formats. ✓ *Pros*: The **high rendering** of PNG files | Images can support a **transparent background** part | Compression does **not cause data loss** ✗ *Cons*: The size of the files is quite **large**
JPEG | .jpeg	This file is called Joint Photographic Expert Group, and is the most widely used. ✓ *Pros*: The size of these files remains **rather small** | Compression allows to optimize the size of the file by slightly reducing the quality, but this type of format allows to be used **on all platforms** (even those with a size limitation) ✗ *Cons*: Images do **not support transparent background** | A **loss of quality** may be felt as backups are made
PDF | .pdf	It is not an image but remains a current file type See previous section

Other formats such as .gif .tiff or .svg are more or **less frequent** depending on your use.